THE EXAMPLE SCHOOL PORTFOLIO

A Companion to

The School Portfolio:
A Comprehensive Framework
for School Improvement

by

Victoria L. Bernhardt, Leni L. von Blanckensee,

Marcia S. Lauck, Frances F. Rebello,

George L. Bonilla, and Mary M. Tribbey

EYE ON EDUCATION
6 Depot Way West, Suite 106
Larchmont, N.Y. 10538

ISBN 1-883001-92-7

Library of Congress Cataloging-in-Publication Data

The example school portfolio : a companion to The school portfolio, a comprehensive
framework for school improvement / by Victoria L. Bernhardt.
     p. cm.
   Includes bibliographical references.
   ISBN 1-883001-92-7
   1. School improvement programs--United States. 2. Portfolios in education--United
States. I. Bernhardt, Victoria L., 1952- II. Bernhardt, Victoria L., 1952-. School
portfolio.

LB2822.82 .E92 2000
371.2--dc21
                                                                      99-056802

Also Available from Eye on Education

THE SCHOOL PORTFOLIO:
A COMPREHENSIVE FRAMEWORK FOR SCHOOL IMPROVEMENT 2/E
by Victoria L. Bernhardt

DATA ANALYSIS FOR COMPREHENSIVE SCHOOLWIDE IMPROVEMENT
by Victoria L. Bernhardt

DESIGNING AND USING DATABASES FOR SCHOOL IMPROVEMENT
by Victoria L. Bernhardt

TECHNOLOGY TOOLS FOR YOUNG LEARNERS
by Leni von Blanckensee

WRITING IN THE CONTENT AREAS
by Amy Benjamin

PERFORMANCE STANDARDS AND AUTHENTIC LEARNING
by Allan A. Glatthorn

PERFORMANCE ASSESSMENT AND STANDARDS-BASED CURRICULA:
THE ACHIEVEMENT CYCLE
by Allan A. Glatthorn

STAFF DEVELOPMENT:
PRACTICES THAT PROMOTE LEADERSHIP IN LEARNING COMMUNITIES
by Sally J. Zepeda

IMPLEMENTATION: MAKING THINGS HAPPEN
by Anita M. Pankake

THE DIRECTORY OF PROGRAMS FOR STUDENTS AT RISK
by Thomas L. Williams

THE PAIDEIA CLASSROOM: TEACHING FOR UNDERSTANDING
by Terry Roberts with Laura Billings

THE INTERDISCIPLINARY CURRICULUM
by Arthur K. Ellis and Carol J. Stuen

COLLABORATIVE LEARNING IN MIDDLE AND SECONDARY SCHOOLS
by Dawn M. Snodgrass and Mary M. Bevevino

TEACHING IN THE BLOCK: STRATEGIES FOR ENGAGING ACTIVE LEARNERS
Edited by Robert Lynn Canady and Michael D. Rettig

Acknowledgements

This book would not have been considered or completed if school portfolio workshop participants had not encouraged us at every workshop to do so. We acknowledge the school personnel who participated in our workshops, especially those who feel the urgency to work in different ways, who see the need to base their curriculum decisions on process and student achievement data, and who desire to see their school operate as a whole and healthy learning organization. We hope this resource helps to make your work easier and your commitment stronger. We acknowledge that this is hard work. The outcomes are worth the dedication, sweat, and tears, however. We thank you for doing this important work for children.

Special thanks to our reviewers from California, Michigan, Missouri, and Ohio, who helped us improve this product. They are: Connie Calloway, Lisa Cayton, Cheryl Cozette, Barbara Gatzulis, Pat Gopperton, Elaine Hassemer, Linda Kakes, Pat Lamson, Mary Ellen Murray, Sheryl O'Connor, Alan Pagano, Anna Phelan, Martha Scott, Janice Wu, Sharon Yates, and Marlene Trapp.

We are indebted to Lynn Varicelli whose attentive and creative work on the layout helped so much to visually portray our ideas. Her dedication to supporting our work is unmatched. A special thanks to Marcy and Tom Lauck for their contributions to the layout. Thank you to our entire staff at the Education for the Future Initiative who help schools do this work every day. And, as always, our Publisher, Bob Sickles, Eye on Education, has been wonderful to work with and incredibly patient.

With gratitude to the SBC and Pacific Bell Foundations who started the Education for the Future Initiative and stuck with it to make it a nationally acclaimed organization. Without their infrastructure and support, we would not have the opportunity to disseminate this work across the country.

And, finally, in appreciation, we dedicate this product to all educators continuously improving their learning environments for students.

About the Authors

Victoria L. Bernhardt, Ph.D., is Executive Director of the Education for the Future Initiative (EFF), sponsored by SBC Foundation in partnership with the Region XI Northern California Comprehensive Center, and Professor in the Department of Professional Studies in Education, California State University, Chico. Dr. Bernhardt is the author of *The School Portfolio: A Comprehensive Framework for School Improvement, Data Analysis for Comprehensive Schoolwide Improvement,* and *Designing and Using Databases for School Improvement,* all published by Eye on Education, 6 Depot Way West; Larchmont, NY 10538; 914-833-0551.

Leni L. von Blanckensee has been an Education for the Future Initiative Associate since 1993. She collaborates with school and school district leaders throughout Northern California to support their reform efforts using school portfolios and data analysis for continuous improvement and conducts workshops throughout the country. During the 1999-2000 school year, Leni went "back to the trenches" to test our theories and is working as a restructuring coordinator and teacher for Paden Elementary School, Alameda, California. Ms. von Blanckensee is the author of the book, *Technology Tools for Young Learners,* published by Eye on Education, 6 Depot Way West, Larchmont, NY 10538, 914-833-0551, which synthesizes some of the the work that resulted from EFF assisting the Pacific Bell Education First Demonstration Sites in integrating telecommunications technology across the curriculum and throughout their organizations.

Marcia (Marcy) S. Lauck, an Education for the Future Initiative Associate since 1995, is engaged in a unique Education for the Future (EFF) partnership with San Jose Unified School District (SJUSD). Marcy's focus in this 33,000 student district has been to help build the District's capacity to support the continuous improvement efforts of all 43 SJUSD schools. Ms. Lauck has worked to strategically align EFF's comprehensive framework for school improvement with the District's quality management emphasis. All schools now annually complete a districtwide climate survey and use the information from students, parents, and staff to assess the quality of their learning environments and set annual goals for improvement. In growing numbers, SJUSD schools create portfolios, assess their programs using the EFF Continuous Improvement Continuums, are engaged in cutting-edge action research based on use of timely data and are creating innovative partnerships to support their global reform efforts. EFF's and SJUSD's shared goal is a seamless integration of school and district efforts to evaluate the effectiveness of SJUSD educational programs and support student learning.

Frances (Fran) F. Rebello worked with Dr. Bernhardt in the induction for the Beginning Teacher Program (IBT) at California State University, Chico (CSUC), between 1986 and 1991. When Dr. Bernhardt went to work with the Education for the Future Initiative and the Pacific Bell Foundation, Ms. Rebello continued to support student teachers at CSUC, which she has done since 1986, and served as a consultant for twenty-four schools in the Chico Unified School District. Part of her responsibility with the district was assisting all twenty-four schools in developing school portfolios. Prior to her work with California State University, Chico, she was a teacher and principal for fourteen years in the San Francisco Bay Area.

George L. Bonilla collaborates with school and school district leaders throughout California and the country to support their reform efforts using school portfolios and data analysis for continuous improvement. He helps build the capacity of schools and districts to do this work through his one-on-one consulting and hands-on workshops on continuous improvement and evaluation, as well as technology-driven data collection and analysis tools. Before becoming an Associate with Education for the Future, George served as a technology coordinator for Juarez-Lincoln Accelerated School in Chula Vista, California. His hands-on approach to teaching educators how to gather, analyze, and use information generated from data for schoolwide improvement has established him as a popular consultant to schools.

Mary M. Tribbey is the Data Coordinator for Butte County Office of Education, Oroville, CA. Ms. Tribbey is currently developing databases for small schools and districts that allow them to examine student achievement data over time and disaggregate it by demographic and programatic data.

Education for the Future Initiative offers School Portfolio, Data Analysis, and Database workshops at the local, regional, state, and national levels.

Authors can be reached through—

Education for the Future Initiative
400 West First Street
Chico, CA 95929-0230
Tel: (530) 898-4482
Fax: (530) 898-4484
http://eff.csuchico.edu

Contents

PART 3 — SUMMARY AND CONCLUSIONS

Foreword

Leading by Example Improves Student Success

The SBC Foundation,[1] along with the Southwestern Bell, Pacific Bell, Nevada Bell, and Ameritech Foundations, has a tradition of leading by example. Through the volunteer work of our employees, the charitable giving arm of the Foundation, and the civic leadership of our company, we have promoted positive change throughout our service territory.

It is our heritage of community leadership that makes us proud to continue our support of the critical work of Victoria L. Bernhardt, a pioneer in education reform. We've supported Dr. Bernhardt and the Education for the Future Initiative for nearly a decade because we believe that through this organization's leadership in education reform, we've helped students achieve academic success. We've seen measurable increases in student achievement in schools across the nation through the efforts of Education for the Future.

The Example School Portfolio, A Companion to the School Portfolio: A Comprehensive Framework for School Improvement encourages schools to commit to and use school portfolios to implement change and increase student learning. In this book, Dr. Bernhardt, and her associates, Leni von Blanckensee, Marcy Lauck, Fran Rebello, George Bonilla, and Mary Tribbey, demonstrate how the School Portfolio clearly spells out the purpose and vision of a school and then measures performance against that vision.

Leading by example through work such as the School Portfolio, the Education for the Future Initiative has been doing what most legislators have only been able to talk about. They have implemented a results-oriented approach to education that focuses on measurable student performance and achievement.

As leaders in our industry and in the communities we serve, we share in the Education for the Future Initiative vision of broadening educational opportunity for every child and increasing the potential for each student to succeed. We hope this book is helpful to educators and school administrators who share that vision.

Gloria Delgado
President
SBC Foundation
San Antonio, Texas

---

[1] The SBC Foundation, along with the Southwestern Bell, Pacific Bell, Nevada Bell, and Ameritech Foundations, is the charitable foundation of SBC Communications and its family of companies, including Pacific Bell, Southwestern Bell, Nevada Bell, SNET, Cellular One, and Ameritech properties.

Preface

The mission of the Education for the Future Initiative[2] is to support and build the capacity of schools to provide an education that will prepare students to be anything they want to be in the future.

The Example School Portfolio, A Companion to the School Portfolio: A Comprehensive Framework for School Improvement is offered to you in the spirit of this mission. The purpose of *The Example School Portfolio* is two-fold. The first purpose is to support the efforts of school personnel as they design and create their own school portfolio. The second purpose is to demonstrate the uses of the school portfolio as a continuous improvement tool.

From our experiences of 10 years, we know that schools committed to using school portfolios have been able to implement systemic changes and student achievement increases in one to two years. With the use of their school portfolios, these schools are able to maintain the changes over time, as well as obtain extramural funding to support the implementation of their visions.

The **secret to the success** of the school portfolio is basically in the implementation of three concepts—
- data-based decision-making
- alignment of everything the school does to a vision that is shared by all the people who make up the learning organization
- documenting the work and results

One of the greatest benefits of the school portfolio is having a place to organize school data in a meaningful way, from demographic data about the school's clients to data about the impact of their school processes on student learning. Used effectively, these data must be organized, kept historically, and must be available to any member of the organization when they want to use it. With the portfolio, members of the organization are able to see how all the parts of the school work together to implement the vision. The portfolio clarifies what needs to change to achieve alignment of the parts to the vision. When all elements of the school are in alignment, one plan can be created to implement the school's vision. Joel Barker (1993) describes in one of our favorite quotes:

> *A vision without action is merely a dream.*
> *Action without vision just passes the time.*
> *A vision with action can change the world.*

---

[2]Education for the Future Initiative is located at California State University, Chico, whose Research Foundation acts as Education for the Future's not-for-profit Fiscal Agent.

We have also found that when schools document where they are and where they want to be, their growth and progress will encourage them to continue implementing change and moving forward. Those who do not document lose track of where they are and what they agreed to do. The school portfolio is the documentation of process, products, and progress. The school portfolio works equally well with high schools, middle schools, and elementary schools.

The Example School Portfolio represents one hypothetical (River Road Elementary) school's approach to building a school portfolio. This school neither began with a totally committed staff nor with the data they needed to make their decision-making purposeful and in alignment with their vision. Over the three years represented in this portfolio, one can see what it took to get the data teachers needed to understand how to meet the needs of all their students, and to understand what processes needed to change to get different results. Readers can also see how easy it is to look in on another school and relate to how they operate. By standing back and looking at the school, one can see clearly what the school could do to make significant changes to get different results. After reading this book, teachers and administrators will look at their own school with new eyes and find those elements that, if pulled into alignment, could make all the difference.

Throughout the book, the authors have written annotations in the margins. At the end of each chapter, we summarize what River Road staff wrote with respect to each section, other things that could be included in that section of a school portfolio, and our recommendations for getting more effective results sooner. In addition, we provide insights about how the sections work together to lead to systemic change, and offer practical advice about how to work with staff to get the work done efficiently and effectively. School personnel can borrow words and ideas, and see how the sections fit together as they create their own sections. Although written about an elementary school, this book is applicable to schools of all grade levels.

On the basis of reading this book and the previously published *The School Portfolio: A Comprehensive Framework for School Improvement*, Second Edition, we encourage you and your school to consider creating a school portfolio, if you do not have one already. If you do have a school portfolio, we hope you find something in this book that will improve and support what you have already done.

Best of luck to you. Feel free to let us know your impressions of *The Example School Portfolio, A Companion to the School Portfolio: A Comprehensive Framework for School Improvement*. We will be continuously improving it.

Sincerely,

Victoria L. Bernhardt
vbernhardt@csuchico.edu

Leni von Blanckensee
lvonb@telis.org

Marcia Lauck
marcy@imagination-at-work.com

Fran Rebello
frebello@csuchico.edu

George Bonilla
bonilla@home.com

Mary Tribbey
mtribbey@edison.bcoe.butte.k12.ca.us

Part 1
Introduction

Chapter 1
The Need for an Example School Portfolio

The Need for an Example School Portfolio

Since the early 1990's, when Education for the Future Initiative schools first began using school portfolios, school personnel have been requesting a book that would describe step-by-step procedures for creating their own school portfolio—a "how-to" book. In response to that request, and to enable the dissemination of the work, *The School Portfolio: A Comprehensive Framework for School Improvement* (Bernhardt, 1994; Second Edition, 1998) was published, and workshops to assist schools in developing school portfolios were (and still are) conducted by Education for the Future Initiative staff.

As a direct result of the school portfolio book and workshops, school personnel became curious to see examples of portfolios created by schools that had successfully used the process. To provide those examples, Education for the Future Initiative staff duplicated excerpts of a few schools' actual portfolios and lugged those heavy binders to their workshops, apologizing to participants because they could only look at the example school portfolios during that workshop session. Occasionally, upon special request, and when a school swore on a stack of portfolios that they would return the examples on a specific day, Education for the Future Initiative staff reluctantly left an example with them. Problems soon developed. When the examples were not returned by the date of the next workshop, participants in that workshop were consequently precluded from seeing the school portfolio example for their schools' grade levels.

To address the obvious need for an example school portfolio that school personnel could keep, Education for the Future Initiative Associates collaborated to produce this book, which can be used to assist school personnel with the development of their own school portfolio. Data from real schools have been used to create this fictitious school portfolio.

The Example School Portfolio is a companion to *The School Portfolio: A Comprehensive Framework for School Improvement.* With these two publications, any school can design and create their own school portfolio. *The Example School Portfolio* is organized around the Education for the Future Initiative Continuous Improvement Continuums. The research behind each of the Continuums is presented in the school portfolio book. The Continuums appear in both *The School Portfolio* and *The Example School Portfolio* books, along with recommendations for using them with staff for measuring your school's progress towards comprehensive schoolwide improvement. An additional publication, *Data Analysis for Comprehensive Schoolwide Improvement,* explains the importance of data and how to effectively gather and use data to make better decisions and to promote systemic change. The methods used to analyze the data shown in this example are displayed in the data analysis book.

What is a School Portfolio?

A school portfolio is a purposeful collection of work that tells the story of a school and the staff's systemic continuous improvement efforts to better serve their clients—the students. The school portfolio clearly spells out the purpose and vision of a school. It measures and ensures congruence of all parts of the organization to enable the implementation of the vision. A school plan and vision are key to moving a school or district towards continuous improvement.

Purposes and potential uses of a school portfolio are to—
- establish one living document that describes an overall school plan and the school's mission, vision, beliefs, and rationale for improvement
- document efforts on a number of elements important to school improvement and align them with the vision
- understand the complexities of the schoolwide organization
- provide readily accessible and necessary information for data-based decision-making
- reflect on progress and purpose
- troubleshoot the continuous improvement efforts of the school
- assess and guide the school's unique approach to continuous schoolwide improvement
- be accountable
- communicate to students, staff, parents, and community
- replace a local, state, or regional accreditation process[3]
- apply for resources

The elements of a school portfolio include the following:
- *Information and Analysis* establishes systematic and rigorous reliance on data for decision-making in all parts of the organization.
- *Student Achievement* supports schools in moving teachers from providers of information to researchers who understand and can predict the impact of their actions on student achievement.
- *Quality Planning* assists schools in developing the elements of a strategic plan including a mission, goals, action plan, outcome measures, and continuous improvement and evaluation.
- *Professional Development* helps staff members, teachers, and principals change the manner in which they work, i.e., how they make decisions; gather, analyze, and utilize data; plan, teach, and monitor achievement; evaluate personnel; and, assess the impact of new approaches to instruction and assessment on students.

---

[3]The School Portfolio is *not* an add-on. It becomes the story of the school and the work behind implementing the vision. Many state and regional accreditation associations are recognizing the benefits of the School Portfolio and allow schools to use it in lieu of their traditional requirements.

- *Leadership* assists schools in thinking through shared decision-making and leadership structures that will work with their specific population, climate, and vision.
- *Partnership Development* assists schools in understanding the purposes of, approaches to, and planning for educational partnerships with business and community groups, parents, other educational professionals, and students.
- *Continuous Improvement and Evaluation* assists schools in further understanding the interrelationships of the components of continuous improvement and in improving their processes and products on an ongoing basis.

The Purpose of This Book

The first purpose of this book is to support the efforts of school personnel as they design and create their own school portfolio. The second purpose is to demonstrate the use of the school portfolio as a continuous improvement tool. School personnel can borrow words and ideas, and see how the sections fit together as they create their own sections. Readers will see how the elements of the school have to be in alignment in order to attain sustainable student achievement increases. Readers will also see how different results can be achieved through an understanding of the impact of the instructional strategies used throughout the school—the school's processes. Feel free to copy the beginning pages of the school portfolio chapters for your beginning pages. (These are the pages that have the Education for the Future Initiative copyright at the bottom of the pages—pages 29, 32, 88, 124, 146, 162, 180, and 208.) You may also request the digital files via our webpage—http://eff.csuchico.edu.

The Organization of This Book

The Example School Portfolio is a prototype of a real school portfolio. The school, River Road Elementary, is fictitious; however, the data and examples come from a number of real schools.

The work revealed in the River Road Portfolio took place over a three-year period. We have divided the work into three parts: Introduction; The River Road School Portfolio; and Summary and Conclusions. Chapter 2 provides an overview of the portfolio and a summary of how the work evolved in the school over the three years. Part 2 which encompasses Chapters 3 through 10 are the River Road portfolio. These sections are organized around the Education for the Future Initiative Continuous Improvement Continuums found in Appendix A of this book. Specifically, those sections and chapters appear as follows:

Chapter 3   Introduction to the River Road School Portfolio
Chapter 4   Information and Analysis
Chapter 5   Student Achievement
Chapter 6   Quality Planning
Chapter 7   Professional Development
Chapter 8   Leadership
Chapter 9   Partnership Development
Chapter 10   Continuous Improvement and Evaluation

On the pages in each of these chapters, the authors have written annotations in the margins which are intended to support you as you build your school portfolio. At the end of each chapter, the authors summarize—

- the progress made by the school during the three-year period and what is driving the results they are getting
- traditional items schools would want to put in that section of their school portfolio
- how the work demonstrated in that particular chapter makes a difference for continuous improvement
- recommendations for working with staff to help them create their own school portfolio efficiently and effectively

Additionally, from the perspective of the authors' practical experiences, you will find insights into each section and how the sections work together with the other sections are shared.

Part 3, Chapter 11, Summary and Conclusions, pulls the River Road Portfolio, a review of the elements of a school portfolio, and the recommendations of the authors together into a conclusive discussion. Appendix A houses the Education for the Future Initiative Continuous Improvement Continuums along with recommendations for their use. Finally, Appendix B shares some mechanics for putting the actual portfolio together. We have tried not to duplicate ideas already provided in *The School Portfolio: A Comprehensive Framework for School Improvement.*

Learn from This Example

Our recommendation to you is to learn from this example. Start your continuous improvement efforts with the school portfolio process and with the commitment of your staff. The Education for the Future Initiative Continuous Improvement Continuums are excellent for organizing your school portfolio, for measuring where your school is right now, and for discussing what evidence you have to demonstrate you are where you think you are.

You will see student achievement increases when all the elements of your school are aligned with your vision, when you have analyzed your data to know the results you are getting now based on current processes, and when you have altered current processes to get different results. Documenting your work through the school portfolio process will make a significant difference in realizing increases in student achievement and implementing systemic change.

River Road is far from a perfect school. It started this process a little haphazardly, but eventually embraced it. See if you can understand how you can get their third-year results by the end of year one. It is possible!

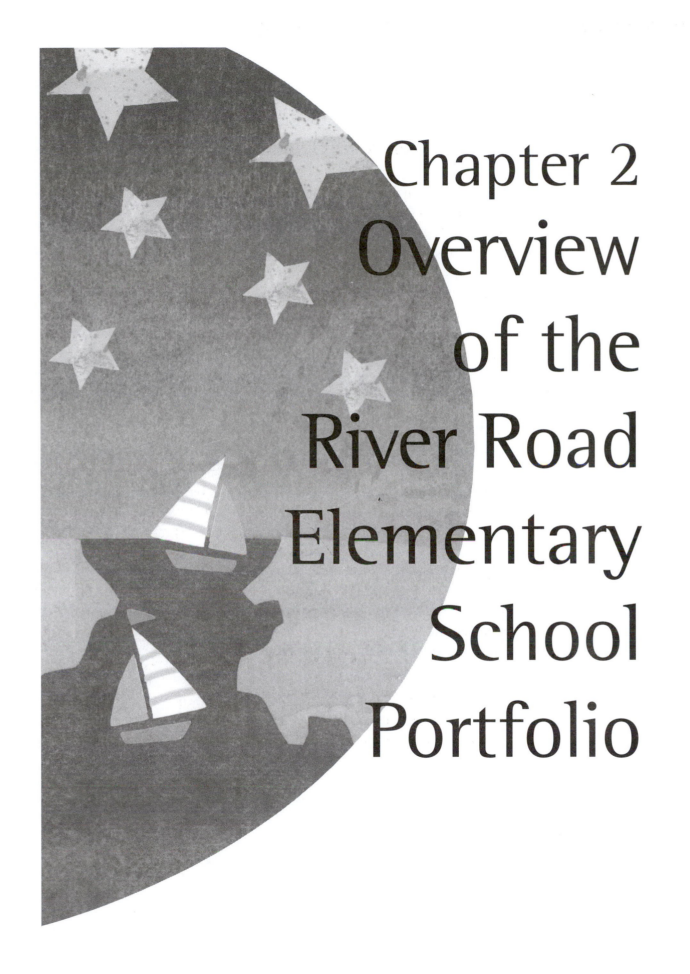

Chapter 2
Overview of the River Road Elementary School Portfolio

Overview of the
River Road Elementary School Portfolio

In the eight chapters that follow is a fictitious school portfolio organized around the Education for the Future Initiative Continuous Improvement Continuums. The portfolio is written as if the teachers of the school, River Road Elementary, have documented three years of their work in this portfolio. In an actual school portfolio of a real school, the narratives would be written by staff members based on input from all staff (this element is further discussed in the Leadership Chapter.) The real school would also include many artifacts showing its work. Examples of artifacts or evidence have been noted throughout this fictitious school portfolio, and some have been created for inclusion in this book.

This chapter presents an overview of how the work of this school evolved over the three years it committed to developing and using the school portfolio process. Additionally, it describes what the school looked like the year before it started using the school portfolio. It projects how this work might evolve in the next two years if the staff continues to progress at the same rate they have worked during the initial three years. Tables 1 through 8 in this chapter display these five years of growth and change. A brief summary of each section of the table follows a short introduction to River Road Elementary School.

Chapter 10, Continuous Improvement and Evaluation, summarizes the River Road staff's assessment on the Continuous Improvement Continuums during the three years of this school portfolio work. It is an excellent summary of the progress and next steps of River Road staff as they progressed over the years. You might want to begin with this chapter if another overview is desired.

Introduction to River Road Elementary School

This brief chapter introduces us to River Road staff's purpose for creating a school portfolio, and sets the context of the change efforts documented in the portfolio.

Information and Analysis

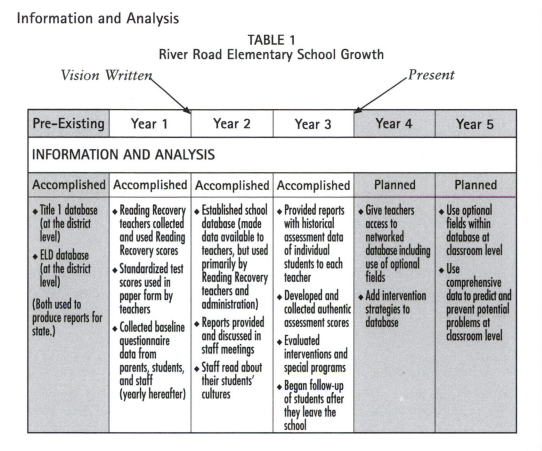

TABLE 1
River Road Elementary School Growth

Vision Written → ← *Present*

Pre-Existing	Year 1	Year 2	Year 3	Year 4	Year 5
INFORMATION AND ANALYSIS					
Accomplished	Accomplished	Accomplished	Accomplished	Planned	Planned
◆ Title 1 database (at the district level) ◆ ELD database (at the district level) (Both used to produce reports for state.)	◆ Reading Recovery teachers collected and used Reading Recovery scores ◆ Standardized test scores used in paper form by teachers ◆ Collected baseline questionnaire data from parents, students, and staff (yearly hereafter)	◆ Established school database (made data available to teachers, but used primarily by Reading Recovery teachers and administration) ◆ Reports provided and discussed in staff meetings ◆ Staff read about their students' cultures	◆ Provided reports with historical assessment data of individual students to each teacher ◆ Developed and collected authentic assessment scores ◆ Evaluated interventions and special programs ◆ Began follow-up of students after they leave the school	◆ Give teachers access to networked database including use of optional fields ◆ Add intervention strategies to database	◆ Use optional fields within database at classroom level ◆ Use comprehensive data to predict and prevent potential problems at classroom level

River Road is a school of over 900 students, with many low income families and a growing immigrant population. River Road became purposeful about the need to work more systemically as a result of two events: first, the superintendent mandated that staff must bring all students up to academic grade level by the end of grade three; and second, shortly thereafter, several staff members attended a school portfolio workshop and saw that using a systemic approach, based on data and documented in the school portfolio, could help them discover how to make the school responsive to the needs of all students.

River Road started building their school portfolio without knowing their clients, which you will witness to be a most critical element in the success in their school's continuous improvement efforts. Like most staff, River Road teachers thought they knew their students and their families, but were surprised when they collected the data and saw the facts. River Road began with very little data of any kind for staff to use to improve their instructional processes. They had standardized test scores and some demographics. Staff and administration used data only in a reactive sense. In other words, data were used to provide reports for district, state, regional, and federal accreditation and funding agencies. The reports were not shared throughout the school. In fact, many reports were created at the district level and never seen by school staff. As staff began their continuous improvement work, they realized data held the answers to many of their questions:

- How and what do we need to improve to increase student learning?
- How can we get all students reading on grade level?
- How do we know if what we are doing is making a difference?

By year two, staff had put together a lot of data, but it was not deep enough or useful for their immediate or long-term needs. From the time staff knew they needed data, to the time they generated the database that would give them all the data they wanted, almost three years had passed. After two-and-a-half years, teachers were able to chart the previous year's standardized test scores and authentic assessment ratings for each of their students. Now, in year four, they are in a position to set goals for the end of the year, work backward to determine where the students should be every month in order to reach the end-of-year goals, and measure monthly to know if they are getting there and to know if they need to adjust instruction for the class or any student. The networked database accessible to teachers enables them to predict and prevent potential student failure.

Schools need this type of database in order to conduct action research, to understand the impact of their processes on student learning, and to be able to predict and prevent student failure. This work requires district support and dollars. If districts can build databases that can also be accessed and used by schools and allocate personnel to help them with this work, the results would be tremendous.

Student Achievement

TABLE 2
River Road Elementary School Growth

Vision Written → *Present* →

Pre-Existing	Year 1	Year 2	Year 3	Year 4	Year 5
STUDENT ACHIEVEMENT *Goal 1—Early Literacy: All students will read at or above grade level by grade three*					
Accomplished	Accomplished	Accomplished	Accomplished	Planned	Planned
◆ Provided Reading Recovery for bottom 20% of grade one (2 teachers) ◆ Piloted literacy groups in grade two	◆ Implemented literacy groups in all grades two ◆ Piloted literacy groups in grade one (2 teachers)	◆ Implemented literacy groups in kindergarten and grades one ◆ Extended Reading Recovery (43 additional part-time teachers) ◆ Examined student writing	◆ Added speech and language screening for students below-grade level before placing in literacy groups ◆ Encouraged all teachers to use Reading Recovery strategies	◆ Implement Reading Recovery strategies in all classrooms	◆ Implement Reading Recovery strategies in all classrooms
Goal 2—Standards and Assessment: Curriculum and assessment will be based on rigorous standards					
◆ Some authentic assessment and student portfolios used in some individual classrooms	◆ Ideas shared by teachers on how student portfolios can reflect language arts standards	◆ Created six-level rubric in writing ◆ Encouraged use of student portfolios	◆ Used student self-assessment through portfolios as part of parent/teacher/student conferences	◆ Align curriculum with standards and assessments	◆ Align curriculum with standards and assessments
◆ Districtwide workshops in student portfolio process	◆ District developed language arts standards	◆ District developed language arts assessments ◆ District developed math standards	◆ District developed math assessments ◆ District developed science standards ◆ District aligned state and local standards ◆ District tied report cards to standards	◆ District will develop science assessments ◆ District will develop social studies standards	◆ District will develop social studies assessments

See Table 3 for Goals 3 and 4

13

TABLE 3
River Road Elementary School Growth

Vision Written   *Present*

Pre-Existing	Year 1	Year 2	Year 3	Year 4	Year 5
STUDENT ACHIEVEMENT (Continued)		*Goal 3—Technology: Technology will be integrated into the curriculum at all grade levels to enhance student learning*			
Accomplished	Accomplished	Accomplished	Accomplished	Planned	Planned
◆ Developed technology plan ◆ Some classrooms had and made use of computers	◆ Provided at least one computer per classroom ◆ Teachers started to share ideas of computer uses in the curriculum	◆ Revised technology plan ◆ Added technology coordinator ◆ Began Tech Wizards in grades four and five ◆ Provided second computer to all classes in grades four and five	◆ District network was established ◆ Technology coordinator began ◆ Technology plan is implemented ◆ Provided second computer to all classes in grades two and three ◆ Extended Tech Wizards to grades four and five	◆ Integrate technology into project-based units ◆ Provide second computer to all classes in kindergarten and grade one	◆ Integrate technology into project-based units across all grade levels
		Goal 4—Hands-on Project-based Instruction: Students will have greater access to the curriculum through hands-on, project-based learning			
◆ District adopted hands-on science program	◆ Implemented project-based science units	◆ District adopted hands-on math program	◆ Math and science project-based units were developed and used	◆ Align Adopt-A-Watershed units to science standards	◆ Implement Adopt-A-Watershed units schoolwide

Staff members at River Road were congenial with one another but pretty much existed in their own isolated classrooms when they began their continuous improvement efforts. Staff knew they needed to change that approach. The teachers' ultimate goal was to begin working together for the benefit of the students by building a continuum of learning that makes sense for all students. During year one, teachers realized they needed data and standards for student performance and assessment to help inform their efforts. They conformed to the district timeline, taking four years to create their baseline standards and assessments. Because they had data for Reading Recovery, the teachers could clearly understand the processes that needed to change to get different results in reading. They made progress with primary reading instruction and achieved positive results.

Quality Planning

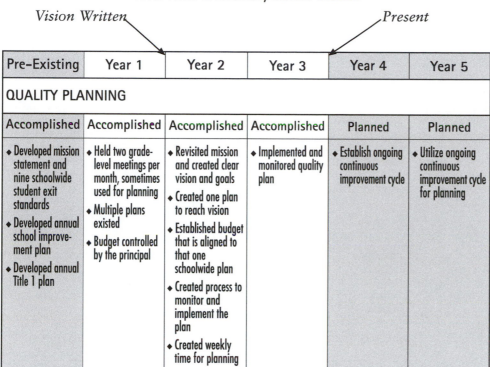

TABLE 4
River Road Elementary School Growth

Vision Written →   *Present* →

Pre-Existing	Year 1	Year 2	Year 3	Year 4	Year 5
QUALITY PLANNING					
Accomplished	Accomplished	Accomplished	Accomplished	Planned	Planned
◆ Developed mission statement and nine schoolwide student exit standards ◆ Developed annual school improvement plan ◆ Developed annual Title 1 plan	◆ Held two grade-level meetings per month, sometimes used for planning ◆ Multiple plans existed ◆ Budget controlled by the principal	◆ Revisited mission and created clear vision and goals ◆ Created one plan to reach vision ◆ Established budget that is aligned to that one schoolwide plan ◆ Created process to monitor and implement the plan ◆ Created weekly time for planning	◆ Implemented and monitored quality plan	◆ Establish ongoing continuous improvement cycle	◆ Utilize ongoing continuous improvement cycle for planning

River Road staff discovered the difference between having a mission statement given to them and developing a mission and vision based on the values and beliefs of the school community. In these same two years of discovery, staff also learned the difference between creating several annual plans and one quality plan that represents the action to get to the vision. With annual plans, it is easy to lose track of the vision and make very little progress. With one quality plan to reach the vision, staff could collapse several action lines into one line and achieve the vision.

15

Professional Development

TABLE 5
River Road Elementary School Growth

Vision Written → *Present* →

Pre-Existing	Year 1	Year 2	Year 3	Year 4	Year 5
PROFESSIONAL DEVELOPMENT					
Accomplished	Accomplished	Accomplished	Accomplished	Planned	Planned
◆ Teachers chose from a smorgasbord of trainings	◆ Trained teachers in a variety of areas	◆ Trained whole staff in shared decision-making process	◆ Trained all teachers to access the school database	◆ Train all teachers to utilize the school database for action research ◆ Use action research findings throughout most grades	◆ Use action research throughout school ◆ Utilize peer coaching in all content areas
◆ Trained two teachers in early literacy ◆ Trained two teachers in Reading Recovery	◆ Trained two additional teachers in Reading Recovery	◆ Trained more classroom teachers in Reading Recovery strategies	◆ Trained all K-3 teachers in Reading Recovery strategies ◆ Began peer coaching in Reading Recovery strategies	◆ Continue to train all K-3 teachers in Reading Recovery strategies ◆ Extend peer coaching for all K-3 teachers in Reading Recovery	◆ Continue and extend peer coaching
◆ Encouraged teachers to take county technology training	◆ Encouraged teachers to take county technology training	◆ Technology coordinator coached individual teachers in the classroom ◆ Provided trainings in Kidpix and Hyperstudio	◆ Technology coordinator coached individual teachers in the classroom ◆ Provided training in e-mail and the Internet	◆ Technology coordinator will coach individual teachers in the classroom ◆ Provided training in integrating technology	◆ Technology coordinator will coach individual teachers in the classroom ◆ Continue training in integrating technology
	◆ Provided training for two teachers in Adopt-A-Watershed (AAW) strategies	◆ Four teachers were sent to AAW leadership training ◆ Trained teachers in hands-on math (district)	◆ Offered AAW training to interested teachers ◆ Grade-level teams shared math/science projects	◆ Offer Adopt-A-Watershed training to all teachers ◆ Use grade-level teams to integrate technology into math/science projects	◆ Continue Adopt-A-Watershed training ◆ Use peer coaching to implement hands-on units

Professional development had always been a first-come, first-served proposition at River Road. Teachers could choose what professional development they wanted to attend unless there was a new program to implement, such as Reading Recovery, then priority would go to Reading Recovery. Professional development evolved through the professional development continuum over the three-year reporting period, and staff ultimately brought in a facilitator who could help them translate their vision into action—working differently, in order to implement a vision and a continuum of learning that makes sense for all students. This professional development training included learning about the culture of their students and creating a professional culture for teachers to learn together for the students. River Road had to make time for peer coaching, action research, and articulation meetings. These processes brought the teachers together to become the consummate professionals they are. It is now the way they do business.

Leadership

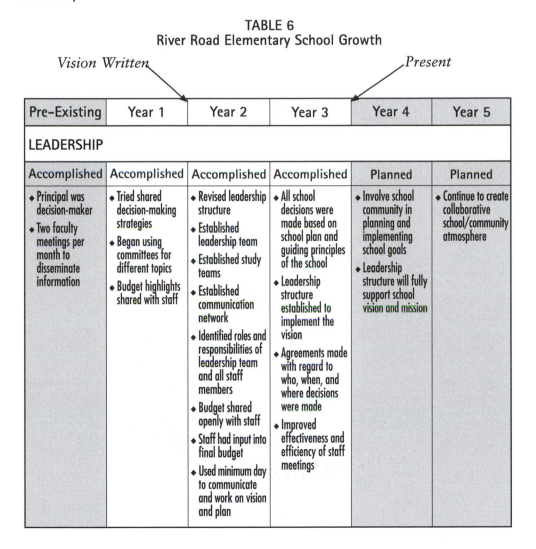

TABLE 6
River Road Elementary School Growth

Vision Written   *Present*

Pre-Existing	Year 1	Year 2	Year 3	Year 4	Year 5
LEADERSHIP					
Accomplished	Accomplished	Accomplished	Accomplished	Planned	Planned
◆ Principal was decision-maker ◆ Two faculty meetings per month to disseminate information	◆ Tried shared decision-making strategies ◆ Began using committees for different topics ◆ Budget highlights shared with staff	◆ Revised leadership structure ◆ Established leadership team ◆ Established study teams ◆ Established communication network ◆ Identified roles and responsibilities of leadership team and all staff members ◆ Budget shared openly with staff ◆ Staff had input into final budget ◆ Used minimum day to communicate and work on vision and plan	◆ All school decisions were made based on school plan and guiding principles of the school ◆ Leadership structure established to implement the vision ◆ Agreements made with regard to who, when, and where decisions were made ◆ Improved effectiveness and efficiency of staff meetings	◆ Involve school community in planning and implementing school goals ◆ Leadership structure will fully support school vision and mission	◆ Continue to create collaborative school/community atmosphere

River Road began the quest to improve what they do for students with a traditional leadership structure. The principal was the decision-maker. With shared decision-making, professional development, and the implementation of the vision, new leadership structures emerged. When the leadership structure began to look like the vision, the shared decision-making and the vision kicked into action. By year three, everything staff did was related to the vision. Staff meetings were about implementing the vision and reviewing measurements. Decisions were made based on the vision and data.

Partnership Development

TABLE 7
River Road Elementary School Growth

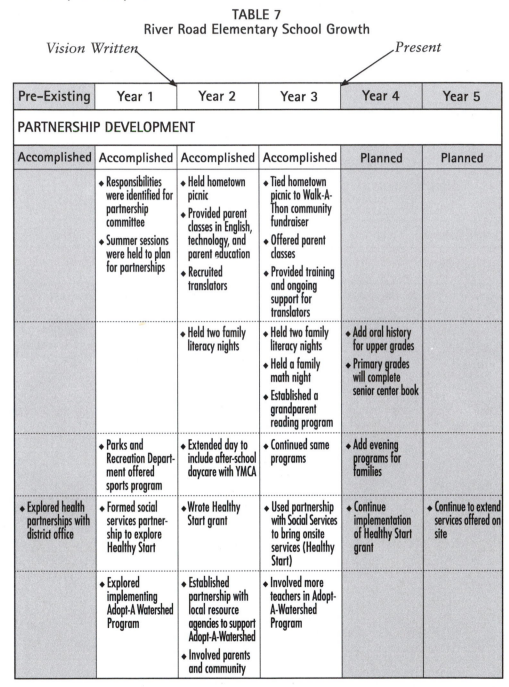

Vision Written   *Present*

Pre-Existing	Year 1	Year 2	Year 3	Year 4	Year 5
PARTNERSHIP DEVELOPMENT					
Accomplished	Accomplished	Accomplished	Accomplished	Planned	Planned
	◆ Responsibilities were identified for partnership committee ◆ Summer sessions were held to plan for partnerships	◆ Held hometown picnic ◆ Provided parent classes in English, technology, and parent education ◆ Recruited translators	◆ Tied hometown picnic to Walk-A-Thon community fundraiser ◆ Offered parent classes ◆ Provided training and ongoing support for translators		
		◆ Held two family literacy nights	◆ Held two family literacy nights ◆ Held a family math night ◆ Established a grandparent reading program	◆ Add oral history for upper grades ◆ Primary grades will complete senior center book	
	◆ Parks and Recreation Department offered sports program	◆ Extended day to include after-school daycare with YMCA	◆ Continued same programs	◆ Add evening programs for families	
◆ Explored health partnerships with district office	◆ Formed social services partnership to explore Healthy Start	◆ Wrote Healthy Start grant	◆ Used partnership with Social Services to bring onsite services (Healthy Start)	◆ Continue implementation of Healthy Start grant	◆ Continue to extend services offered on site
	◆ Explored implementing Adopt-A-Watershed Program	◆ Established partnership with local resource agencies to support Adopt-A-Watershed ◆ Involved parents and community	◆ Involved more teachers in Adopt-A-Watershed Program		

River Road genuinely evolved in the way they sought and worked with partners. They used to bemoan the fact that parents and the community were not beating down the doors to help them. They were also unhappy that businesses were not dropping large bundles of dollars on their doorstep. The sad fact was that if either of these phenomena had occurred, they would not have known what to do with these resources. There was no vision and there was no plan.

As staff learned about planning for a vision, they learned to include planning for partnerships. With standards for student learning identified, they could plan to include partners who could contribute to the vision. They also learned that by knowing what their partners needed out of the partnership, they could build mutually strong relationships.

Continuous Improvement and Evaluation

TABLE 8
River Road Elementary School Growth

Vision Written   *Present*

Pre-Existing	Year 1	Year 2	Year 3	Year 4	Year 5
CONTINUOUS IMPROVEMENT AND EVALUATION					
Accomplished	Accomplished	Accomplished	Accomplished	Planned	Planned
◆ Gathered required data	◆ Began putting data together to understand where the school was	◆ Used baseline data to understand needs and develop vision and plan	◆ Used data to evaluate plan and drive improvement ◆ Brought data to the teacher level	◆ Use data to evaluate plan and drive improvement	◆ Use data to evaluate plan, drive improvement, and prevent student failure
Information and Analysis	Approach 1 Implementation 2 Outcome 2	Approach 3 Implementation 3 Outcome 3	Approach 4 Implementation 4 Outcome 4		
Student Achievement	Approach 1 Implementation 1 Outcome 1	Approach 3 Implementation 3 Outcome 2	Approach 4 Implementation 4 Outcome 3		
Quality Planning	Approach 1 Implementation 1 Outcome 1	Approach 3 Implementation 3 Outcome 3	Approach 4 Implementation 4 Outcome 4		
Professional Development	Approach 2 Implementation 2 Outcome 2	Approach 3 Implementation 3 Outcome 3	Approach 4 Implementation 4 Outcome 4		
Leadership	Approach 1 Implementation 1 Outcome 1	Approach 3 Implementation 3 Outcome 3	Approach 4 Implementation 4 Outcome 3		
Partnership Development	Approach 1 Implementation 2 Outcome 1	Approach 3 Implementation 3 Outcome 3	Approach 4 Implementation 4 Outcome 4		
Continuous Improvement and Evaluation	Approach 1 Implementation 1 Outcome 2	Approach 2 Implementation 2 Outcome 2	Approach 4 Implementation 4 Outcome 4		

The Education for the Future Continuous Improvement Continuums (CICs) were lifesavers for River Road staff. The continuums helped them know where they were when they started, where they were headed, and where they were at the times they did their assessments. The CICs also helped them know the difference in the *approach* they were taking to each continuum, whether or not they were truly *implementing* that approach, and the *outcome* they were getting (details of assessing with the CICs are found in Chapter 10). Just when staff would begin feeling burdened by the hard work of continuous improvement, it was time for another assessment. Each time they assessed, they saw progress which kept them moving ahead. The other thing that the Continuous Improvement Continuums did for them was to help them keep everything in their learning organization in alignment with the vision. The Continuous Improvement Continuums helped them focus on next steps. Overall, with a committed staff, they made consistent and very good progress.

Part 2
The River Road
School Portfolio

Chapter 3
Introduction
to the
River Road
Elementary
School
Portfolio

NOTES

Begin your School Portfolio with an attractive cover that invites people to learn about your school.

Welcome

to the

River Road Elementary

School Portfolio

Riverview Unified School District
Riverview, California

RIVER ROAD ELEMENTARY

SCHOOL portfolio PORTFOLIO

The River Road Elementary School Portfolio

Our River Road school portfolio was developed to document the changes and progress our school has made while working to continuously improve everything we do. The portfolio provides our staff with an ongoing means for self-assessment, communication, continuous improvement, and accountability.

The categories used in this portfolio are based upon the Education for the Future Initiative Continuous Improvement Continuums, adapted from business' Malcolm Baldrige Award Program for quality business management and achievement. These categories were selected because we agree that the philosophies written into the continuums will lead to River Road becoming a quality school. Within each category is a description of the intent of the category, a brief summary of where we are as a school, and our next steps.

The seven categories utilized in this school portfolio are—
- Information and Analysis
- Student Achievement
- Quality Planning
- Professional Development
- Leadership
- Partnership Development
- Continuous Improvement and Evaluation

This school portfolio is a living document that describes River Road and includes actual evidence of our work. It describes who we are, our vision for the school, goals, plans, progress, and achievements in the context of client demographics and needs, and school partnerships. The portfolio also describes how we build and utilize our overall school plan for the purpose of increasing student learning—our ultimate outcome. The last section, Continuous Improvement and Evaluation, summarizes our three years of assessments on the Continuous Improvement Continuums. It is in this final chapter that one can see an

SCHOOL **portfolio** PORTFOLIO

NOTES

The Continuous Improvement Continuums are located in Appendix A of this book along with recommendations for their use.

overview of all the progress and changes we have been able to accomplish within each section and throughout our school during this time. It also shows how all of the parts fit together to make our school a positive place for our students.

A team of teachers were involved in developing the narrative for our portfolio based on input from the whole staff. Much of the narrative content came from discussions of the staff in the process of evaluating our work using the Continuous Improvement Continuums. During these bi-yearly assessments, staff were also asked to contribute "evidence" of our progress—actual documents that show the changes in our practices.

Please enjoy this comprehensive treasure as it provides the "big picture" of who we are, how we evolve over time, and interrelate to prepare students to become successful citizens and participants in their future world!

The Staff of
River Road Elementary School

THE SCHOOL PORTFOLIO

garden

*A school portfolio is like a garden—
It takes planning and hard work,
requires the weeding out
of unnecessary elements,
and promotes positive feelings.
You're proud to show it off!*

photograph album

*A school portfolio
is like a photograph album—
It brings back memories
for the people involved,
shows changes over time,
and introduces people to thinking
in ways they have
never thought before.*

master's painting

*A school portfolio
is like an old master's painting—
It captures the school's essence, and yet,
a closer look reveals
interesting details.
The more you study it,
the more you see.*

wise friend

*A school portfolio
is like a wise friend—
It listens, clarifies your ideas,
and is something
you don't want to lose.
Most of all, it provides insight
to help you create your future.*

Many People of Education for the Future, 1994

Chapter 4
Information and Analysis

Introduction to Information and Analysis

Today's problems come
from yesterday's solutions.

Peter Senge

Schools committed to improvement must collect and analyze data in order to understand:

- the current and future needs of the school, students, parents, teachers, and community
- how well the current processes meet the needs of these clients
- the ways in which the school and community are changing
- root causes of problems
- the types of education programs and expertise that will be needed in the future

Schools that utilize and analyze information about the school community make better decisions about what to change and how to institutionalize systemic change. Research shows that schools that understand the needs of their clientele are more successful in implementing changes and remain more focused during implementation than those schools that do not identify specific needs. Information and analysis works hand-in-glove with comprehensive school improvement, and is a critical element in planning for and determining the effectiveness of change.

Types of information and analyses that assist with planning for and sustaining systemic school improvement include demographics, assessment of current and desired practices, perceptions of the learning environment, student achievement data, and problem analysis.

Note. From *The School Portfolio: A Comprehensive Framework for School Improvement,* Second Edition (p.27), by Victoria L. Bernhardt, 1998, Larchmont, NY: Eye on Education: Copyright © 1998 Eye on Education, Inc. Reprinted with permission.

SCHOOL **portfolio** RTFOLIO

Information and Analysis

While the other sections of the River Road school portfolio show all three years of information, this section on Information and Analysis was revised each year so that the previous year's data would be included in graphs with the current year's data. This makes sense for our staff since we want to watch our growth and be able to use historical data to predict and prevent student failure. The story of our progress with Information and Analysis is reported in summary in this chapter.

Information and analysis contents are as follows:

- Overview of River Road Elementary School
- Riverview Unified School District
- The Community of Riverview
- River Road Staff
- River Road Students
    Mobility
    Families
    The Hmong
- Questionnaire Results
    Students
    Staff
    Parents
- Student Achievement
    The Evolution of Our Use of Data at
    River Road

SCHOOL **portfolio** PORTFOLIO

NOTES

It is important to lay out the story of the school, its district, and its community.

In a "real" school portfolio, the writers would indicate the year the portfolio was started and the current year— to ground the reader.

Overview of River Road Elementary School

River Road Elementary School is a kindergarten through grade five public school built in 1952 that currently houses 947 students and 46 instructional staff members. It is one of 10 elementary schools in Riverview Unified School District. River Road is located on the outskirts of Riverview, California, right

next to the Nodaway River. On one side of the river is the main part of the city, a traditional blue-collar neighborhood, where students live in older tract homes, now mostly rented, and in newer low income public housing apart-ments. On the other side of the river, are families from a combination of small trailer park communities and older homes located on the edge of town and through the agricultural community that supports the city's canneries.

The staff at River Road have seen the character and ethnic distribution of the students change fairly dramatically over the past five years, and have seen the school population grow to a number that is very difficult to support in the existing facility.

River Road has participated in a statewide program of class size reduction (K-2) for the past two years. The average class size schoolwide is 24. Kindergarten classes include 20 or fewer students; grades one and two are all combination classes of 20 students or fewer; and grades three through five classes are 28 or fewer. River Road's current enrollment configuration by grade level is as follows:

Grade K	158	Grade 3	158
Grade 1	155	Grade 4	164
Grade 2	164	Grade 5	148

SCHOOL **portfolio** PORTFOLIO

Riverview Unified School District

River Road Elementary is part of the Riverview Unified School District which serves approximately 18,000 students in 10 elementary schools, two middle schools, two high schools, a continuation high school, a home study program, and an independent study program. Per capita income in the area served by the district has never been high, but has decreased over time to $15,800, with 11 percent of the total general population and 36 percent of the district's student population living below poverty level. In the last five years, there has been a net 30 percent increase in food stamp recipients and more than a 100 percent increase in the number of individuals receiving non-AFDC medical assistance.

Substance abuse is on the rise in a growing number of homes, and the impact of that abuse has been noticed by teachers in the primary grades. They now refer greater numbers of families to Child Protective Services than they did in the past, and have noticed increasing learning difficulties among children entering kindergarten.

Over the past decade, the demographics of the students in the district have rapidly changed, reflecting the influx of new residents, many of whom are immigrants, and represent the growing minority population in California's urban and rural areas. As a consequence, the district has and still faces additional challenges:
- The minority student population has increased from 10 percent to 40 percent, while the teaching staff has remained predominantly Caucasian.
- Many new residents are recent immigrants, who need additional support services, including language acquisition programs.
- The transiency rate of the district's students has increased from 15 percent to 45 percent.

The Community of Riverview

Riverview, California, is a mid-sized city that has enjoyed a semi-rural existence for many years. The population of this community is changing, however. Families from an increasingly impacted urban area, located approximately 60 miles away, have been moving to Riverview in increasing numbers. Professional families who do not wish to raise their children in an urban environment see Riverview as an attractive alternative. They are willing to commute, and are building homes north of town. Low income families, fleeing living expenses

NOTES

While thoroughly describing your community, you can begin to think of new partnerships and support for the school vision.

Information about your community can be obtained from:
- *Census Bureau*
- *County Offices*
- *Chambers of Commerce*
- *Websites*

SCHOOL PORTFOLIO

The school cannot be a service to the community or to its children, if the adults in the school do not understand who the students are, and the context of the families and cultures from which they come.

they can no longer afford, are also moving to the area. Major employers in the area are two local canneries, several small service businesses, a small mall, the telephone and utility companies, the schools and local community college, city government, and one small technology manufacturing company.

The community offers potential resources and strengths. A community college is located approximately 20 miles north of the city, and has an active partnership with the high schools in Riverview. In addition, Everystate University, located twenty-five miles away, has partnerships with the County Office of Education and neighboring school districts, and provides both preservice teacher preparation and ongoing professional support. There is a small airport on the other side of town, which is currently used primarily for private aircraft. In response to interest shown by companies wishing to relocate to the area, the city council generated redevelopment funding through a bond issue and built an industrial park. The infrastructure of streets, sidewalks, storm drains, and utilities is almost complete, and it is hoped that this will attract high-tech manufacturing businesses that will elevate the local economy and provide partnership opportunities for the area schools.

River Road Staff

River Road has 39 regular classroom teachers, four Reading Recovery specialists (three of whom also teach morning kindergarten), two special education resource teachers, and one special day-class teacher. It also has a technology coordinator who works with teachers in the classrooms. The majority of teachers are

veterans from the pre-demographic change days, having been at the school for six or more years. In the minority are new teachers that were added to reflect the increasing numbers of students attending the school. Although there has been some turnover in the ranks, no key leaders have been lost in the past two years. Indeed, the stability of its staff has been one of the school's strongest points.

SCHOOL portfolio PORTFOLIO

NOTES

Several of the classroom teachers have been trained in Reading Recovery techniques, and in year three, those teachers are now beginning to integrate Reading Recovery strategies into their regular classroom instruction. Many of the teachers, 26 percent, are certified to teach English language learners. All teachers strive to create a classroom climate that is nurturing and conducive to learning for students.

Information and Analysis needs powerful statements of who your staff and students are.

River Road Students

Two years before we began our school portfolio, Caucasian students made up 75 percent of the population, with the remaining 25 percent spread over a variety of ethnicities, including a small but stable population of Hispanic and African-American students and a new population of Hmong and Mien students.

In the past, the bulk of the Caucasian students belonged to blue-collar working class families mentioned previously. Although their numbers have remained fairly stable, the percentage of Caucasian children coming from lower income families has increased over the last 10 years as families moved out and new families moved in. This has been especially true over the past five years. The numbers of Hmong students reflect the most dramatic shift in the student population, and present a special challenge to the staff at River Road. The chart on the next page (Figure 1) represents the change in enrollment by ethnicity over the past five years. (Years one, two, and three are portfolio years. The two years prior to our first portfolio year is noted as "minus two years" and the year before we started our portfolio is noted as "minus one year".)

SCHOOL **portfolio** RTFOLIO

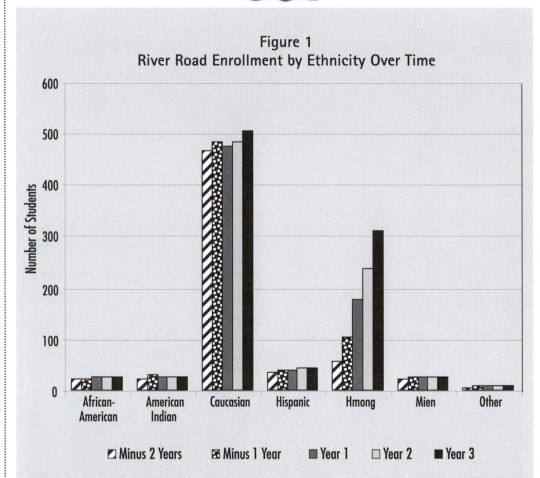

Figure 1
River Road Enrollment by Ethnicity Over Time

As one can see from this chart, the overall population has increased from low 600s to 947 in just five years. The number of African-American, Caucasian, Hispanic, Mien, and "Other" students has remained about the same. The overall increases can be attributed to the addition of Hmong students and families into the community.

At the present time, there are 504 Caucasian, 310 Hmong, 43 Hispanic, 28 Mien, 28 American Indian, 25 African-American, and nine "Other" children at River Road, as shown in the pie chart (Figure 2) on the next page.

SCHOOL **portfolio** PORTFOLIO

NOTES

It is important to analyze the data. It is equally important to present the results clearly in a graph or table so everyone can see the data in the same way. It is also important to describe the results that are presented so there are no misinterpretations.

Eight years ago, there were no Hmong or Mien students at the school. From that time to year three, the number of Hmong students has increased from 54 to 310, while the percentage of Hmong students compared to the total student population has increased from 9 percent to 33 percent. In general, the teachers find Hmong parents unusually attentive and supportive of their children. In spite of that, these students have proven to be a challenge to the staff. The majority of these new families are non-English speaking when they arrive, and neither the children nor their parents have had much of any formal education. Of 158 new kindergartners, 65 arrived at school with few or no skills in English.

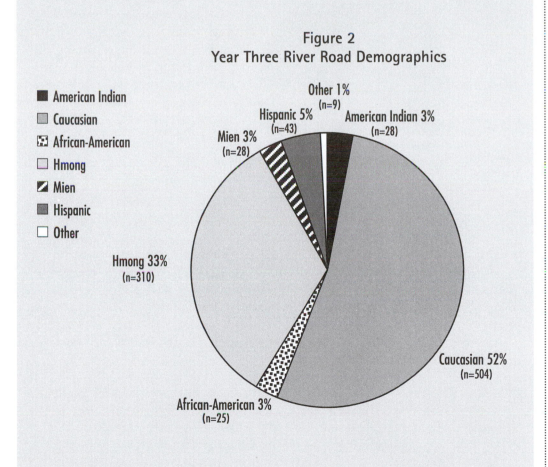

Figure 2
Year Three River Road Demographics

- ■ American Indian
- □ Caucasian
- ▨ African-American
- □ Hmong
- ▧ Mien
- ■ Hispanic
- □ Other

Other 1%
(n=9)

Hispanic 5%
(n=43)

American Indian 3%
(n=28)

Mien 3%
(n=28)

Hmong 33%
(n=310)

Caucasian 52%
(n=504)

African-American 3%
(n=25)

SCHOOL **portfolio** RTFOLIO

Mobility

The River Road student population has become increasingly mobile. Figure 3 identifies the numbers and percentages of the student population that fall within three different groups; those who have been here continuously, those who are new to the school, and those who were here in the past and are returning. Fewer than one-half of the students at River Road have been enrolled continuously since they began their studies here. We disaggregated the mobility groups by ethnicity, and found that there is no difference in pattern between the two largest groups of students—the Caucasians and the Hmong.

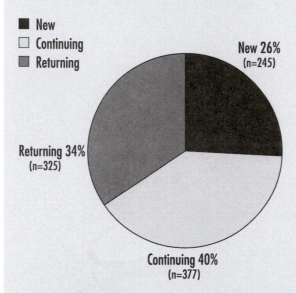

**Figure 3
Student Mobility Year Three**

■ New
□ Continuing
■ Returning

New 26%
(n=245)

Returning 34%
(n=325)

Continuing 40%
(n=377)

Our Families

Many of River Road's students come from poor economic environments, where both immigrant and non-immigrant families must deal with survival issues and may have little time to devote to their children's education. Nearly 25 percent are from homes with only one parent or guardian; 20 percent live in multiple-family homes or apartments where it is common for one family to share a single bedroom. The district's community liaison estimates that 80 percent of its parents work long hours and thus have little time to spend with their children.

Teachers perceive that many students have low self-esteem, poor critical-thinking skills, and lack the readiness needed for success in school which they partly attribute to a lack of time with parents, some of whom have inadequate parenting skills. Many students at River Road have special needs that are not met in traditional school structures and programs.

SCHOOL *portfolio* RTFOLIO

River Road has not received benefits from the urban flight of professionals. Eighty-nine percent of our students are eligible for Title 1 services, and 93 percent of the children benefit from either free or reduced priced lunches. Approximately 85 percent of River Road parents are not college educated, and many have not finished high school. Many of the families that have lived in the area the longest can be characterized as working poor, working seasonally for the local canneries, and supplementing that income the rest of the year as best they can. The small number of parents who own small businesses, work at the university, continue to work small family farms, or work in offices downtown tend to be the school's most active parents.

The Hmong

For all these years that we have had Hmong students in our school, we thought we knew all about their culture. Last year, a couple of teachers were on the Internet looking for strategies for working with the Hmong. They ran across the history of the Hmong and shared it with all the staff. It was at that time that all River Road teachers began to look at these children and their families a little differently. What we discovered made us ashamed that we had not taken the time and effort to understand earlier the impact of history on our children and their families. Knowing more about their culture made all the difference in the world to us. It changed the way we think, act, and teach. Continued on the following page is part of what we learned. (Excerpt reprinted with permission from Jeff Lindsay, Appleton, Wisconsin.)

http://www.athenet.net/~jlindsay/Hmong_tragedy.html, http://www.hmongnet.org/

The Hmong in the U.S. came mainly from Laos as refugees after the Vietnam War. They once lived idyllic agrarian lives in the hills of northern Laos, but that changed once many of them were recruited by the CIA to fight for us in the once-secret wars in Laos. They fought bravely and suffered many casualties, but once we pulled out from Vietnam and left them in the lurch, the North Vietnamese and their puppet government in

Numeric data is essential to understanding who the clients are and how the school can better serve their needs. Descriptive data can also be extremely valuable, as demonstrated by the information about the Hmong found on the Internet and included in the River Road Elementary School Portfolio.

Pictures help personalize the portfolio and bring it to life.

LAOS

SCHOOL portfolio PORTFOLIO

Truly understanding who the students are can change the way a school operates. To meet each student's needs, the staff must take into account the prior experience including the family and cultural context which each child brings to the learning environment.

Laos marked the Hmong for genocidal extinction. Many of the Hmong fled from invaders (and from chemical weapons, including "yellow rain" and other toxins), losing many lives as they traveled through the jungle and swam the Mekong river to Thailand.

Every Hmong family I have met here can tell of blood-chilling stories of escape or of the awful deaths of loved ones. It seems like everyone lost a mother, father, brother, sister, or spouse during the war and during the escape to Thailand and the U.S. The stories told by young people, describing what they experienced at age four or five are especially chilling.

The Hmong are different and highly misunderstood. Part of the problem is that many Americans do not realize how the Hmong got here. Many think they are just flooding our borders to get welfare benefits.

There are roughly 150,000 Hmong people in the U.S., largely concentrated in Wisconsin, Minnesota, and California. Several million Hmong people remain in China, Thailand, and Laos, speaking a variety of Hmong dialects. The Hmong language group is a monosyllabic, tonal language (seven to twelve tones, depending on the dialect). The written language is said by some to have been eradicated over centuries of persecution in China (though it is not certain that there ever was a unique written language for Hmong). According to some traditions, Hmong women once sought to preserve their banned Hmong writing by stitching stylized characters into their dresses. Some of the symbols may have been preserved, but their meaning was lost. It was not until late in this century that a writing system for Hmong was introduced. Several forms were attempted, but the dominant method is a romanization system in which pronunciation seems highly nonintuitive for English and Hmong speakers alike, though it seems to be based on sound linguistic principles. An increasing number of materials have been printed in the romanized Hmong language, but it is still difficult for most of the Hmong people to read.

Hmong refugees in the U.S. struggle with our unusual ways, though the rising generation of youth have melted in well with American culture, even at the risk of losing touch with their heritage. For the older generation, adopting the new ways has been painful. The

SCHOOL **portfolio** RTFOLIO

language is a great barrier to the elderly, many of whom have had no schooling and had no reading skills prior to coming to the U.S. Simple things like going to a store or walking through town can be terrifying experiences for the elderly.

Our teachers cried when they read the story of the Hmong, and we then understood that our other immigrant and minority students had similarly painful histories. We wondered how our culture could become so insular. We cried even harder when we read about the Hmong children achieving in other locations in the United States. The language and family income barriers can no longer be an excuse.

SCHOOL **portfolio** RTFOLIO

Education for the Future questionnaires have been used extensively by schools across the country for collecting students', teachers', and parents' perceptions. Copies of Education for the Future questionnaires appear in the Appendices of "The School Portfolio: A Comprehensive Framework for School Improvement" and "Data Analysis for Comprehensive Schoolwide Improvement." We invite schools to use them.

In order to conduct analyses over time, it is necessary that the instrument used to collect the data be reliable and valid. When selected or designed, it is important to keep the questions as well as the instrument's scale (e.g., 1 to 5 points) constant so comparisons can be made over time.

Questionnaires

Starting at the end of school year one, River Road staff began administering questionnaires to students, parents, and ourselves. These questionnaires helped us see who we are and how our clients perceive the learning environment we are providing for our students.

We learned a lot about administering and analyzing questionnaires during these three years. Luckily, in the first year, we had a person who knew how to make the questionnaires readable with a scanner. The hands-on data analysis workshop some of us attended ultimately helped us learn how to gather and analyze data electronically, allowing us to cut out printing costs and get completed questionnaires returned. We also learned to administer questionnaires to parents when the majority of parents are at the school.

In the first year of collecting questionnaire data, River Road did not think perceptions of students, staff, and parents would be a strong component of our data analysis process. (By the end of year three we had a different opinion.) The school had, in the past, sent questionnaires to parents, taken informal staff questionnaires, mostly during staff meetings, and usually on a subject not associated with student achievement. River Road staff looked at Education for the Future's questionnaires and decided to adopt them to help the school expedite the process of collecting strong perceptions data. A team from River Road reviewed the questionnaire items to ensure that all items in all three questionnaires were applicable to River Road's environment. During the review of the questionnaires the survey team learned more about questionnaire development using *Data Analysis for Comprehensive Schoolwide Improvement* as a resource. This was an important step because these questionnaires will be used over time, and once data are collected, the items should not be changed. If the items do change, one cannot see improvements in attitudes from one year to the next. To this end, the River Road survey team made sure that their questionnaire instruments were:

- valid
- reliable
- understandable
- quick to complete
- able to get the first response from the respondent
- able to get what they wanted in the end

SCHOOL **portfolio** PORTFOLIO

At the conclusion of the River Road survey team's evaluation of the Education for the Future's questionnaires, the following guidelines for questionnaire administration were developed:

- The questionnaires will remain unchanged.
- The questionnaires will be administered in the computer lab for staff and students, and will be printed for parents and hand carried to the parents, by the students.
- Enthusiasm will be promoted among all staff and students to achieve maximum return of questionnaires. Tips for teachers on how to create enthusiasm among their students will be shared by the survey team.
- Designated staff (with help from parent volunteers) will be trained to administer the questionnaires in the computer lab, and to collect and chart the data.
- A timely turn around time for processing the questionnaires and reporting the results to all clients (student, parents, and staff) will be established and adhered to.

Each of the questionnaires hosted a five-point scale, 1 being strongly disagree and 5 being strongly agree. The questionnaire results were charted on a line chart for the three years, showing the average response for each item for each year.

NOTES

How large should our sample be? Your reasons for administering the questionnaire in the first place can help answer this question. For example, in assessing the feelings and views of staff members, it might not be acceptable to sample, even though, statistically speaking, a sample would be adequate. You want to hear from every staff member and they usually want to be heard as well. Not giving them the opportunity would cause some people to feel left out and possibly to be suspicious of bias in the data. The bottom line is that in collecting perceptions data from such important constituencies as parents, students, and staff, there is absolutely no good reason to not go for a 100% return rate.

SCHOOL **portfolio** PORTFOLIO

Those teachers not willing or unable to share questionnaire results with their students, in a positive and meaningful way, should not be involved. The principal or data team members can share the information with students for those teachers who do not feel comfortable with this task.

Even with a modest computer lab, schools should be able to get 100% of the students to respond to the questionnaires. Two or three staff members familiar with the online administration of questionnaires can provide direction for the students and help expedite the process of taking questionnaires in the lab.

Student Questionnaires

River Road staff administered the Education for the Future student questionnaire three years in a row. The averages for the three years are shown in Figure 4. As one can see from the chart, each year all item averages fell into the agree and strongly agree categories. All item averages increased over the three years, with the exception of two items, the differences of which were negligible. Those items were:

- My principal cares about me
- My family wants me to do well in school

In both cases, the year-two results were slightly higher than the year-three results.

The consistently highest scoring items over the three years were—

- My family wants me to do well in school
- My teacher is a good teacher
- My family believes I can do well in school
- My teacher believes I can learn
- My teacher cares about me
- My teacher treats me with respect
- I can be a better student

The item averages that increased the most from year one to year three were (in order of the greatest gains):

- I have fun learning
- Students at my school treat me with respect
- I have lots of friends
- Students are treated fairly by the people on yard duty
- I have support for learning at home
- My teacher believes I can learn
- My teacher treats me with respect
- I am a good student

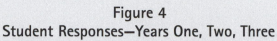

SCHOOL PORTFOLIO

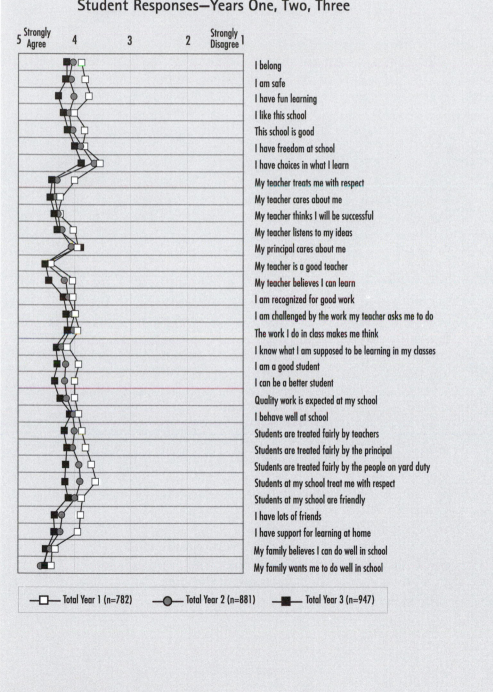

Figure 4
Student Responses—Years One, Two, Three

5 Strongly Agree	4	3	2	Strongly Disagree 1

I belong
I am safe
I have fun learning
I like this school
This school is good
I have freedom at school
I have choices in what I learn
My teacher treats me with respect
My teacher cares about me
My teacher thinks I will be successful
My teacher listens to my ideas
My principal cares about me
My teacher is a good teacher
My teacher believes I can learn
I am recognized for good work
I am challenged by the work my teacher asks me to do
The work I do in class makes me think
I know what I am supposed to be learning in my classes
I am a good student
I can be a better student
Quality work is expected at my school
I behave well at school
Students are treated fairly by teachers
Students are treated fairly by the principal
Students are treated fairly by the people on yard duty
Students at my school treat me with respect
Students at my school are friendly
I have lots of friends
I have support for learning at home
My family believes I can do well in school
My family wants me to do well in school

—□— Total Year 1 (n=782)   —●— Total Year 2 (n=881)   —■— Total Year 3 (n=947)

Schools can see how their improvement efforts impact perceptions of the school by using the same questionnaire over time as an essential measurement tool.

Information about designing questionnaires, as well as examples of Education for the Future questionnaires, can be found in "Data Analysis for Comprehensive Schoolwide Improvement" (Appendices A and B). For further information, check the Education for the Future website: http://eff.csuchico.edu

SCHOOL **portfolio** PORTFOLIO

NOTES

It is important to have a well-designed parent questionnaire. The baseline questionnaire will be used over time (i.e., next year and the next) to help observe trends and changes.

Frequently, schools send questionnaires home for the purpose of collecting data related to the requirements of a grant or state recertification, etc. Questionnaires can also assist with meaningful dialog that can actually contribute to comprehensive schoolwide improvement.

Parent Questionnaires

The logistics of developing the parent questionnaire was planned this way— First, the questionnaire items were reviewed to ensure that all items were applicable to our parents/families. Second, because we had a large number of immigrant families we translated the questionnaires to the primary language of the families. We sought the assistance of parents to this end. Third, our team made sure that alignment with the student and parent questionnaires, in some areas, was obtained. For example, *I feel welcome at my child's school* aligned with *I feel like I belong at this school* in both the student and parent questionnaires.

Finally, in order to maximize the return of parent questionnaires, it was necessary that the River Road survey team and principal promote genuine enthusiasm among the staff and students. This was accomplished when the principal and survey team became convinced that the process of data collection and analysis can and will assist them in making better decisions to increase student achievement.

In year one, the parent questionnaire was printed, along with a cover letter to all parents were sent home with the students. By the end of year three, we were administering the parent questionnaires in the computer lab, just like we did the student and staff questionnaires. We determined that parent-teacher conferences were the best times to get the majority of parents into the school. By taking advantage of those times, we could administer the questionnaires and get an excellent response rate.

Overall, parents have been positive in their responses over the last three years. This may indicate an overall satisfaction with the school. The results certainly did not signal that parents are in strong agreement with all school practices that were being addressed by the questionnaire, however. In year one, the following items were lowest:
- I feel welcome at my child's school
- There is adequate playground supervision during school
- There is adequate supervision before and after school
- The school meets the academic needs of the students
- The school has an excellent learning environment

SCHOOL portfolio PORTFOLIO

Perceptions such as the ones listed above had to be addressed and next steps communicated, promptly, to parents. An honest and strong effort was made to include parents on the analysis team for the parents' survey analysis. Their perspective was important to understanding their thinking and perceptions.

An important response that was addressed by the staff and parents who comprised the survey analysis team was *I feel welcome in my child's school.* The team felt this was important to address simply because all parents must be welcome and feel welcomed in the school. A telephone tree was established and teachers called parents to request clarification on this item. After collecting these data, using a preplanned phone interview, the teachers analyzed the results and found that a significant number of parents felt the school's front office was not always receptive to parents and was outright hostile in some cases. The phone interview also found that a few teachers did not seem interested in sharing meaningful information about student progress with parents. In a few cases, the parents felt slighted by the teachers.

The results of this follow-up survey was shared with the entire staff and the following action was taken:

- All staff met to talk about this issue, and brainstorm ways to make parents feel welcome in all parts of the school.
- Two staff members volunteered to research ways of creating an effective, welcoming environment in all parts of the school.
- All staff, including front office personnel, will be inserviced on the virtues of good public relations.

It was evident that related to parent involvement addressing the issues, it made a difference in the year two and year three results. Looking at Figure 5, one can see that by year three, all parent items were in agreement or strong agreement.

NOTES

It is imperative that once questionnaire data have been collected and analyzed, results be reported to all clients. This must be done within a short period of time after questionnaires have been returned to the school. Letters can describe the results of the questionnaire, items identified by staff to be addressed, and school plans for addressing these items. This can become an opportunity to invite parents to participate in the process to resolve issues that could be affecting student learning.

SCHOOL **portfolio** RTFOLIO

Acknowledging the parent community value in schoolwide improvement efforts should be addressed in a well-written cover letter expressing a clear purpose for the questionnaire. Shortly after the questionnaires have been analyzed, another letter communicating the results must be sent to all parents. Parents must be invited to participate in addressing items of concern identified by the questionnaire results.

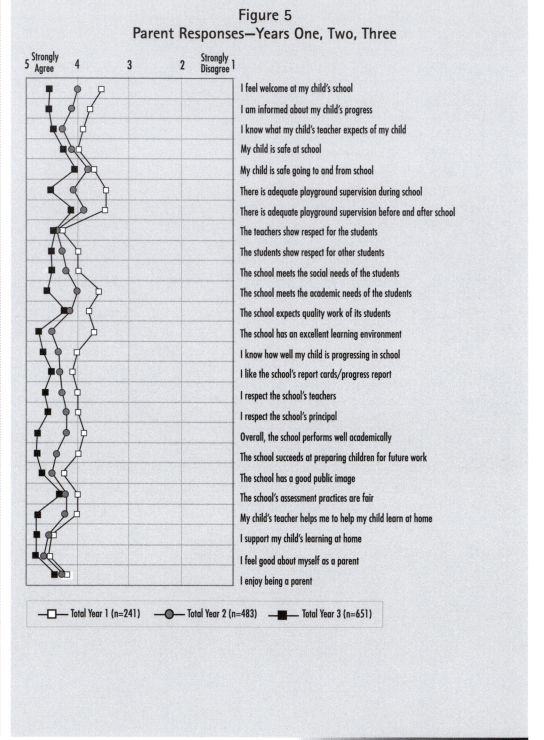

Figure 5
Parent Responses—Years One, Two, Three

5 Strongly Agree 4 3 2 Strongly Disagree 1

I feel welcome at my child's school
I am informed about my child's progress
I know what my child's teacher expects of my child
My child is safe at school
My child is safe going to and from school
There is adequate playground supervision during school
There is adequate playground supervision before and after school
The teachers show respect for the students
The students show respect for other students
The school meets the social needs of the students
The school meets the academic needs of the students
The school expects quality work of its students
The school has an excellent learning environment
I know how well my child is progressing in school
I like the school's report cards/progress report
I respect the school's teachers
I respect the school's principal
Overall, the school performs well academically
The school succeeds at preparing children for future work
The school has a good public image
The school's assessment practices are fair
My child's teacher helps me to help my child learn at home
I support my child's learning at home
I feel good about myself as a parent
I enjoy being a parent

—□— Total Year 1 (n=241)   —●— Total Year 2 (n=483)   —■— Total Year 3 (n=651)

SCHOOL **portfolio** RTFOLIO

NOTES

"Not to understand another person's way of thinking does not make that person confused."
Michael Quinn Patten

Staff Questionnaires

The staff questionnaire was taken each year by all staff members during a staff meeting. The results of all three years appear in Figure 6.

As one can see from the chart, the staff had a lot to work on over the three years. In year one, the staff was neutral to the following items:
- Morale is high on the part of teachers
- We have an action plan in place which can get us to our vision
- The vision for this school is clear
- The vision for this school is shared
- My administrator supports shared decision-making
- My administrator is effective in helping us reach our vision

By the end of year three, all average responses to the items in the staff questionnaire fell solidly in the high agree and strongly agree categories. At the end of year three, all staff said they strongly agree (all 5s) with the following items:
- I believe student achievement can increase through providing a threat-free environment
- I believe student achievement can increase through addressing student learning styles
- I believe student achievement can increase through effective parent involvement
- I believe student achievement can increase through effective professional development related to our vision
- My administrator is effective in helping us reach our vision

SCHOOL portfolio PORTFOLIO

NOTES

It might be necessary to have staff training sessions for all staff to refresh or acquire chart reading skills before the data is shared. Perhaps this chart reading skill building session could be part of a more comprehensive set of sessions designed to build skills in basic statistics, questionnaire familiarization, chart reading, and data analysis. The Vine Concept has proven successful in school sites where time and funding for professional development has been an issue. The process could go as follows: Set up a vine by agreeing on who the vine Keeper or person-in-charge will be. This person should be an energetic, dynamic, respected, (and not-afraid-to-get-involved), staff member. This person may or may not be the principal.

(Continued)

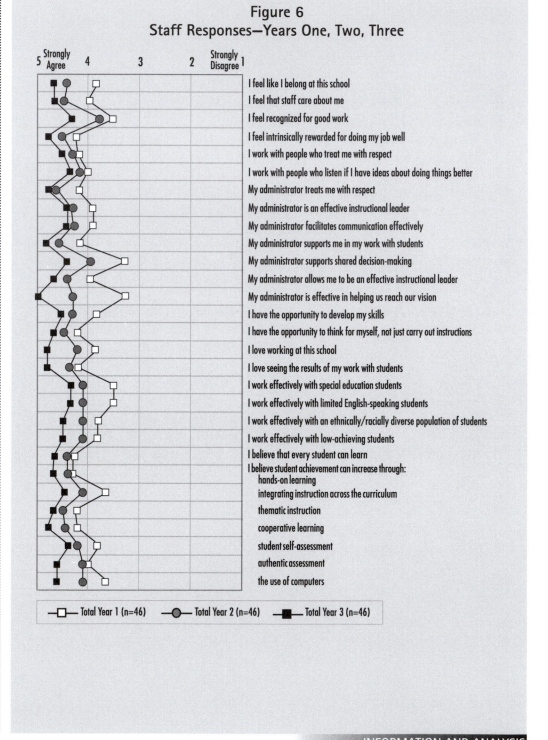

Figure 6
Staff Responses—Years One, Two, Three

SCHOOL portfolio PORTFOLIO

Figure 6 (Continued)
Staff Responses—Years One, Two, Three

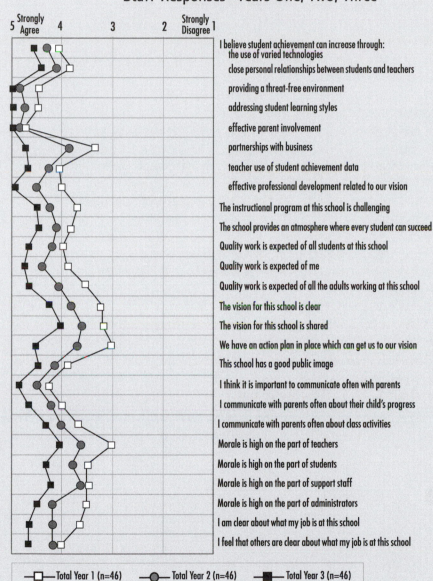

Response	Statement
	I believe student achievement can increase through: the use of varied technologies
	close personal relationships between students and teachers
	providing a threat-free environment
	addressing student learning styles
	effective parent involvement
	partnerships with business
	teacher use of student achievement data
	effective professional development related to our vision
	The instructional program at this school is challenging
	The school provides an atmosphere where every student can succeed
	Quality work is expected of all students at this school
	Quality work is expected of me
	Quality work is expected of all the adults working at this school
	The vision for this school is clear
	The vision for this school is shared
	We have an action plan in place which can get us to our vision
	This school has a good public image
	I think it is important to communicate often with parents
	I communicate with parents often about their child's progress
	I communicate with parents often about class activities
	Morale is high on the part of teachers
	Morale is high on the part of students
	Morale is high on the part of support staff
	Morale is high on the part of administrators
	I am clear about what my job is at this school
	I feel that others are clear about what my job is at this school

Scale: 5 Strongly Agree 4 3 2 1 Strongly Disagree

Legend: Total Year 1 (n=46) — Total Year 2 (n=46) — Total Year 3 (n=46)

Next, all staff members are divided into small groups or vines. Staff members should be grouped based on comfortability in working with each other, access to one another, break times, early birds, late workers, proximity, and anything else which brings people together.

The vine leaders coordinate training activities with the vine keeper. Each vine leader will be responsible for learning a particular concept as directed by the vine keeper, and then teaching the learned concept to the member immediately in the vine below her/him and so on. (Continued)

SCHOOL portfolio PORTFOLIO

NOTES

The vine leaders, as well as the vine keeper, must actively participate in the process. The vine leader will make sure, by keeping in communication with her/his vine, that the target date to finish the training at hand will be met.

The success of each vine depends on how well each member meets their responsibilities for learning and training. Once vine leaders report that a particular training task has been accomplished, the vine leaders and vine keeper will meet to update the training vine and to agree upon the next learning task.

(Continued)

Other items that were almost 5s by the end of year three were:

- My administrator supports me in my work with students
- My administrator treats me with respect
- I think it is important to communicate often with parents
- I feel intrinsically rewarded for doing my job well
- Quality work is expected of all the adults working at this school
- Quality work is expected of me
- I am clear about what my job is at this school
- I feel that others are clear about what my job is at this school
- I believe student achievement can increase through cooperative learning
- I believe student achievement can increase through thematic instruction
- I believe student achievement can increase through partnerships with business
- I love working at this school
- I love seeing the results of my work with students
- I have the opportunity to think for myself, not just carry out instructions
- I believe that every student can learn
- I believe student achievement can increase through "hands-on" learning
- I work with people who treat me with respect
- I feel like I belong at this school
- I feel that the staff cares about me

These item responses are indications that we have a vision that is truly shared with a leadership structure that is supporting the implementation of the vision.

SCHOOL **portfolio** PORTFOLIO

Overall

It is time to acknowledge and celebrate these improvements. The staff has been doing a great job, not only in collecting perceptions data, but also in analyzing the data, addressing the items that the data show must be addressed, and taking corrective action.

This proactive hard work is paying off for the school as a whole. More positive perceptions of students towards their learning environment is being reflected in other areas such as student learning and parent and community perceptions. We know now that our attitudes had to change first!

Following is an example

of a training vine:

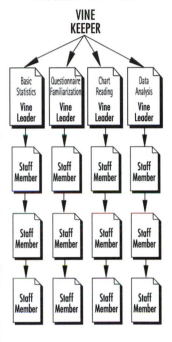

Training Vine
Process Flow Chart

SCHOOL **portfolio** PORTFOLIO

NOTES

Documenting progress on the road to change is a valuable effort, for the staff will see there has been tremendous progress.

Student Achievement

The Evolution of Data Use at River Road

We might have been slow to convince, but when we saw the benefits of having actual data, our staff did everything they could to get individual student achievement records into a historical database that the administration and teachers could access. Teachers now add performance assessment data to the database as the assessments are completed. What follows is a summary of our evolution with data.

Year One

Up to and through year one, teachers primarily relied on classroom level assessment and standardized test scores (CTBS) which were provided in paper form. Two of our teachers attended a workshop in the middle of year one in which they became convinced of the value of having a student achievement database, and of gathering student perceptions about the school and their learning. The whole staff was willing to give it a try, so we did two things. We had the students and teachers complete perception questionnaires, and we sent the teacher who was most knowledgeable about technology to a follow-up, hands-on data analysis workshop.

Year Two

At a faculty meeting in the early fall of year two, our teachers received the individualized test scores for all of our students who had been at the school the previous year. As a group, we also reviewed a series of charts that had been prepared from the same scores, beginning with the schoolwide average normal curve equivalent (NCE) in each area. Then we looked at the same responses by grade, and by grade and gender.

In spite of minor differences from one group to the next, what we saw indicated a pattern that all of our students were performing far below where we wanted them to be performing. Looking at the data this way confirmed our belief that we need to do more of this work to really find out what is happening with the students. We also discussed the baseline results from the student, staff, and parent questionnaires, and what kind of impact they might have on student achievement. We wished we had more time and more expertise!

SCHOOL **portfolio** RTFOLIO

Our unofficial technology coordinator began work on our school's database in year two. Because she was doing this in addition to her regular job as a teacher, and her other job as our official technology mentor, progress was slow. But it was steady. With the help of the district technical support person, she figured out how to get the basic student information from the attendance system. That gave us each student's birthdate, gender, ethnicity, date of enrollment, home language, current teacher, and some program information. By the end of the year, she was able to link the student information to the standardized test scores.

The lead Reading Recovery specialist had been gathering data on the students in the program from the beginning and had gradually added more student scores. In year one, she began to gather data from each of the grade one students, so that she would have comparative information. In year two she asked the grade three, four, and five teachers to continue to gather text-level scores in their classes, so that we could see how the students were doing long-term. All of her data had been recorded on paper, so in year two we had a parent volunteer enter that data into the database so that we could use it with the other data in our database. At this time we were also working with the district committee to develop grade level standards, and made sure that the standards and assessments that we adopted were entered into our database design.

Beginning of Year Three

At the staff retreat held at the beginning of year three, teachers were provided with reports that listed individual students in their classes. This year, the reports included three years of historical standardized test scores for as many students as had them. We also reviewed charts from the database that showed us how the students who had scores for two or more years were doing. It was during this year that we discovered a data querying software tool that allowed us to simply point and click to look at different combinations and disaggregations. Figure 7 on the following page shows the Total Reading NCE average for the past three years, for students in grades three, four, and five during the year two school year. We were pleased to see this chart and the growth that it represented.

An automatic data querying tool is necessary if schools want teachers to really use data. This tool must be point and clickable so teachers can manipulate the data themselves. (This is opposed to having to program different configurations.)

SCHOOL **portfolio** PORTFOLIO

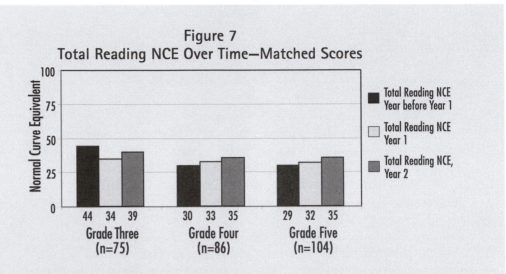

Figure 7
Total Reading NCE Over Time—Matched Scores

In addition to the historical data for the students who had scores for more than one year, we reviewed standardized test-score charts that showed all of the students who took the test last year. This year we were able to break out the students' performance by subscore. What we saw was that grade two students were doing slightly better than the other grades, especially in vocabulary, but that our students were extremely low throughout the school.

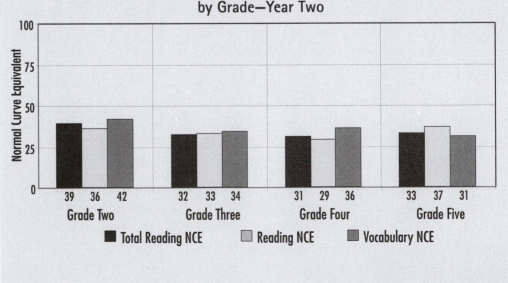

Figure 8
Total Reading, Reading Subscore, and Vocabulary Subscore
by Grade—Year Two

SCHOOL **portfolio** RTFOLIO

We were so thrilled with the ability to look at the scores as graphics, we kept disaggregating the data. As Figure 9 illustrates, looking at the scores by grade and gender, we saw that while there wasn't a big difference between the grade two boys and girls, there was a boy-girl difference in the other grades. The grade three boys were especially low.

Figure 9
Total Reading, Reading and Vocabulary NCE Scores
by Grade and Gender—Year Two

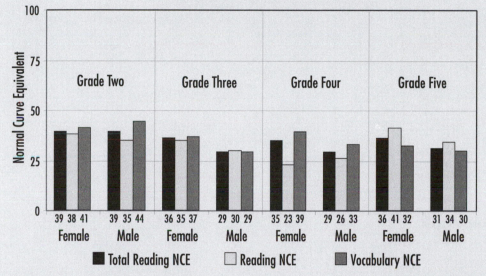

NOTES

The disaggregation of student achievement data helps staff get to the root causes of problems.

River Road Elementary School might have looked more closely at their grade three program to see if teachers were employing instructional strategies that serve the needs of boys as well as girls. School-process (e.g. instructional strategies) data helps the staff understand why they are getting the results shown in the student achievement data.

SCHOOL portfolio PORTFOLIO

NOTES

Charts and tables are included in this section so that the reader can "see" the process.

We also had tables for each of the charts, so that we could see the detail. Table 9 below shows average total reading, language, and math NCE scores and numbers in each category by gender. Here, we noticed that the boys in grades three and four scored quite a bit lower in all three measures than the others.

Table 9
Total Reading, Language, and Math NCE Scores and Numbers by Gender and Grade Level—Year Two

Grade Levels	Gender	Total Reading NCE Year 2	Total Language NCE Year 2	Total Math NCE Year 2	Number of Reading Scores	Number of Language Scores	Number of Math Scores
Grade Two	F	39.1	39.1	43.1	71	72	72
	M	39.2	39.2	44.9	52	55	55
	Average	39.1	39.1	43.9	123	127	127
Grade Three	F	35.5	35.5	37.0	91	90	90
	M	28.8	28.8	30.4	82	82	82
	Average	32.4	32.4	33.9	173	172	172
Grade Four	F	35.1	35.1	36.5	65	65	65
	M	28.8	28.8	29.6	83	81	81
	Average	31.5	31.5	32.7	148	146	146
Grade Five	F	35.9	35.9	43.6	92	91	91
	M	30.5	30.5	32.4	99	99	99
	Average	33.1	33.1	37.8	191	190	190
	Total Average	33.7	33.7	36.7	635	635	635

Because the charts provided to us this year included historical test data and we were able to look at more detail than the previous year, the conversations staff had at the retreat were much more meaningful. We still had work to do, though. The work done at the district level, to decide the other measures of assessment to use, was finished. But, we were not yet gathering those measures in our classrooms and did not yet have them in our database, so we couldn't compare them to the standardized test scores at that time. We wanted to be able to do the same things with the authentic assessments that we had started to do with the standardized test scores.

SCHOOL 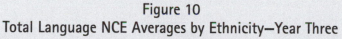 PORTFOLIO

NOTES

We have included many more charts than most schools would include in their portfolio. However, schools that use data will go through this process of examining the data, disaggregated in many ways, in order to find root causes of problems, or to decide which charts are most helpful for discussion.

During year three, we piloted the process of gathering the other measures of assessment and we did have our moments! By the end of the year, though, we were well on our way to having measures for each student at each grade level, and were scoring our authentic assessments more consistently. Now, we have alternative measures of assessment, and we can tie assessment to processes. In most cases, we only had a year's worth of alternative assessment scores for year three, but it was a start, and we were excited. The database was beginning to give us real information. Our technology coordinator was very proud of herself and we were happy until she told us that the district had offered her a full-time position that paid more money and that she had decided to accept. This taught us to always make sure that more than one person learns a process in the future.

End of Year Three

At the end of year three, we received the results from the standardized testing the district had chosen to continue in addition to the state required Stanford Achievement Test (SAT 9). The charts shown below and on the page following (Figures 10 and 11) look at our students on a schoolwide basis. This year's results tell us that our students did better

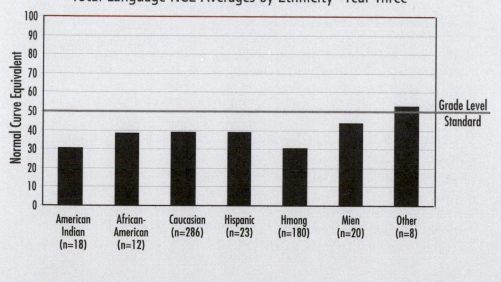

Figure 10
Total Language NCE Averages by Ethnicity—Year Three

SCHOOL **portfolio** PORTFOLIO

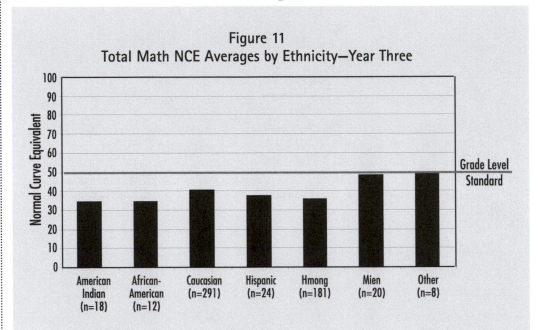

Figure 11
Total Math NCE Averages by Ethnicity—Year Three

in math than in language and that, in general, our African- American, Caucasian, Hispanic, and Mien students are closest to meeting the grade-level standard of 50 NCE in language, although all but one of the averages shown are below 50. That average relates to the "Other" ethnic subcategory representing eight students. Our Hmong students have the lowest averages of the minority students for language, but have a slightly higher average in math than the American Indian and African-American students.

Looking at the NCE averages for reading, language, and math by gender, we found a slight difference between the boys and girls. The average NCE for girls was slightly higher in Total Reading and Total Language and slightly lower in Total Math (see Figure 12).

Looking at NCE averages for reading, language, and math by both ethnicity and gender, we found that only the Caucasian, Hmong, and Hispanic students were present in large enough numbers that we felt we could use their averages to discuss program impact on different ethnic groups (see Figure 13). Numbers are shown on the next page in Table 10. Examining assessment data for students in the smaller groups on an individual basis could still tell us what we could do to best meet their needs.

SCHOOL portfolio PORTFOLIO

NOTES

Disaggregation of student achievement data helps the school know whether the program is serving the needs of all groups of students.

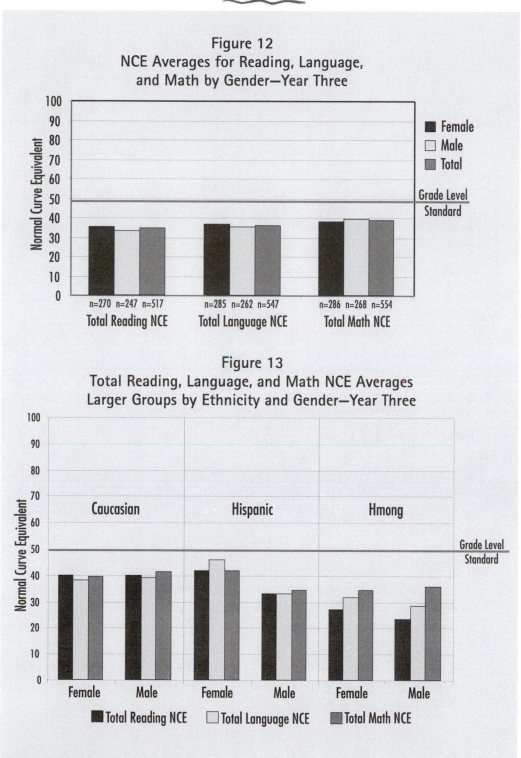

Figure 12
NCE Averages for Reading, Language, and Math by Gender—Year Three

Figure 13
Total Reading, Language, and Math NCE Averages
Larger Groups by Ethnicity and Gender—Year Three

SCHOOL **portfolio** PORTFOLIO

NOTES

The tables help us see the number of students in each group. It is very difficult to get all of these data into a chart.

Table 10
Total Reading, Language, and Math NCE Averages and Numbers
Larger Groups by Ethnicity and Gender—Year Three

Ethnicity	Gender	Total Reading NCE Year 3	Total Language NCE Year 3	Total Math NCE Year 3	Number of Reading Scores	Number of Language Scores	Number of Math Scores
American Indian	Female	25.8	30.2	32.3	10	10	10
	Male		30.0	35.9	8		8
African-American	Female	35.7	42.2	33.7	6	6	6
	Male	24.5	34.0	34.7	6	6	6
Caucasian	Female	40.1	37.9	39.3	143	153	153
	Male	39.8	39.1	41.3	123	133	138
Hispanic	Female	41.8	46.1	41.9	9	10	10
	Male	33.0	33.2	34.2	13	13	14
Hmong	Female	27.0	31.5	34.6	91	95	96
	Male	23.5	28.2	36.0	81	85	85
Mien	Female	36.4	44.4	42.3	7	7	7
	Male	40.2	43.2	51.2	12	13	13
Other	Female	59.5	64.0	60.8	4	4	4
	Male		40.5	37.3	4		4
	Total Average	**34.4**	**35.8**	**38.6**	**517**	**547**	**554**

Table 10 shows that by looking at just the larger groups of students, we found the following:

- The male Caucasian average in Total Language was higher than the female average.
- There was virtually no difference in Total Reading but Total Math mirrored the group gender results.
- The female Hispanic averages were consistently much higher than the male averages.
- The gender differences between Hmong males and females mirrored the group results, but the differences were greater in Total Reading and Total Language.

SCHOOL portfolio PORTFOLIO

Year Three by Grade Level

To move the discussion to grade-level teams, we next disaggregated the average NCEs by grade level (see Figure 14 and Table 11).

Figure 14
Total Reading, Language, and Math NCE Averages
by Grade—Year Three

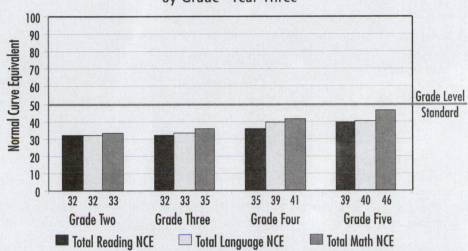

Table 11
Numbers of Students by Grade
for Reading, Language, and Math Scores
Year Three

Grade Levels	Number of Reading Scores	Number of Language Scores	Number of Math Scores
Grade Two	133	144	144
Grade Three	131	131	134
Grade Four	131	146	148
Grade Five	122	126	128
Total Numbers	517	547	554

SCHOOL **portfolio** PORTFOLIO

A Problem Solving Cycle similar to the one described in "Data Analysis for Comprehensive Schoolwide Improvement" (Chapter 9), can help get all staff involved in determining what data to collect and in reviewing the data when it is gathered and analyzed.

The grade five students were closest to our goal, overall. Although they were lower than we would like them to be, we were not surprised by the grade two and grade four averages. However, we had expected the grade three Total Reading and Total Language averages to be higher than they were and were surprised by those averages.

We disaggregated the grade level averages by ethnicity and found a consistent difference in the performance between the two largest groups, the Caucasian and Hmong (Figure 15). We also looked at the other groups, but again found that they were so small that the differences were reflective of individual students rather than the group (see Table 12).

The Total Reading and Total Language averages for Caucasian students were consistently higher than the Hmong students. The Total Math averages for grade two and grade five students were very similar, while the averages for the grade three and grade four students were similar to the reading and language averages.

We also disaggregated the averages by grade and gender and did not find a consistent difference in the performance between the boys and girls (not shown).

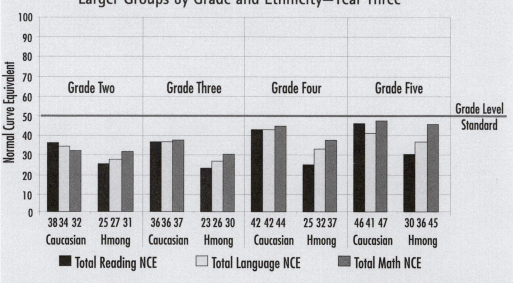

Figure 15
Total Reading, Language, and Math NCE Averages
Larger Groups by Grade and Ethnicity—Year Three

SCHOOL **portfolio** TFOLIO

Table 12
Number of Students by Large Ethnicity Groups and Grade Level for Reading, Language, and Math Scores
Year Three

Grade Levels	Ethnicity	Number of Reading Scores	Number of Language Scores	Number of Math Scores
Grade Two	Caucasian Hmong	63 51	67 58	67 58
Grade Three	Caucasian Hmong	65 40	64 41	66 42
Grade Four	Caucasian Hmong	76 42	88 42	90 42
Grade Five	Caucasian Hmong	62 39	67 39	68 39

NOTES

The data analyses that result from the Problem Solving Cycle similar to the one described in "Data Analysis for Comprehensive Schoolwide Improvement"" (Chapter 9) can lay to rest some old thinking about why a school is getting the results it is getting.

Year Three by Mobility

Next, we disaggregated the NCE averages for year three by whether the students were new to the school, continuing from a previous year, or were returning to the school after being absent for a period of time. This disaggregation revealed that the "new" and "continuing" students had the highest averages (see Figure 16 and Table 13). Students who have been at the school (continuing students) averaged highest in all areas, especially in math.

The returning (theoretically the most mobile), students were approximately five points lower in reading and language, and were eight points lower in math than the continuing students.

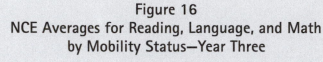

Figure 16
NCE Averages for Reading, Language, and Math by Mobility Status—Year Three

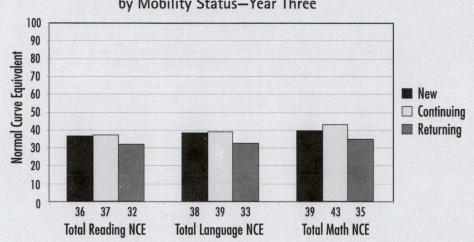

Table 13
Number of Students by Mobility Status for Reading, Language, and Math Scores Year Three

Mobility Status	Number of Reading Scores	Number of Language Scores	Number of Math Scores
New	59	60	62
Continuing	212	226	229
Returning	246	261	263

When we looked at those categories disaggregated by the larger ethnic groups, we learned that the continuing Hmong average was closest to the Caucasian average in Total Math, but were consistently lower in all other categories (see Figure 17 or Table 14). In looking at these categories disaggregated by grade, we discovered that we have very few continuing students in grades two and three. (Table 15).

SCHOOL **portfolio** RTFOLIO

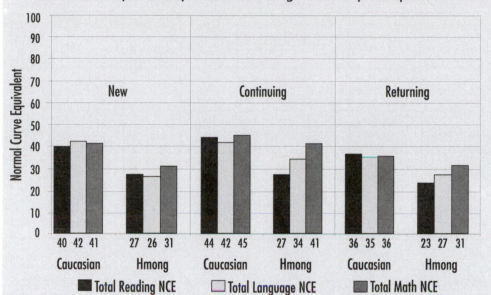

Figure 17
Total Reading, Language, and Math NCE Averages
Schoolwide by Mobility Status and Large Ethnicity Groups—Year Three

NOTES

When schools disaggregate and find out there are many students who are not continuing students, they need to determine how to serve this population, after understanding more about their mobility.

Table 14
Number of Students by Mobility Status and Large Ethnicity Groups for Reading, Language, and Math Scores—Year Three

Mobility Status	Ethnicity	Number of Reading Scores	Number of Language Scores	Number of Math Scores
New	Caucasian Hmong	29 16	29 16	31 16
Continuing	Caucasian Hmong	110 75	123 75	125 75
Returning	Caucasian Hmong	127 81	134 89	135 90

SCHOOL portfolio RTFOLIO

Table 15
Total Reading, Language, and Math NCE Averages and Numbers Schoolwide by Grade and Mobility Status—Year Three

Grade Level	Mobility Status	Total Reading NCE Year 3	Total Language NCE Year 3	Total Math NCE Year 3	Number of Reading Scores	Number of Language Scores	Number of Math Scores
Grade Two	Continuing	37.0	24.8	31.8	4	4	4
	New	32.1	31.7	29.3	15	16	16
	Returning	32.0	32.3	33.3	114	124	124
Grade Three	Continuing	40.7	50.5	40.3	3	2	3
	New	33.3	36.3	36.1	20	20	20
	Returning	31.0	31.8	34.9	108	109	111
Grade Four	Continuing	35.5	38.7	41.4	111	123	124
	New	35.6	45.4	44.2	8	9	10
	Returning	31.7	36.6	34.7	12	14	14
Grade Five	Continuing	38.4	39.3	45.4	94	97	98
	New	44.7	43.7	49.6	16	15	16
	Returning	35.6	37.4	44.2	12	14	14

We tried to look at the averages for our two larger groups, by mobility. In some cases, the numbers are so small that again we are looking at individual students. Although we could not see patterns in test scores this way, we found the numbers of continuing, new, and returning students very informative. The number of reading scores for each group (number of students) is shown below and detailed in Table 16.

- In grade three, there are very few continuing Caucasian students and no continuing Hmong students.
- The largest groups in grade three are Caucasian and Hmong returning.
- In grade two, there are only four continuing Caucasians and no Hmong continuing.
- We are clearly looking at a more mobile population in the lower grades than in the upper grades.

SCHOOL **portfolio** RTFOLIO

Table 16
Number of Students by Ethnicity, Mobility, and Grade Level for Reading, Language, and Math Scores

Grade Level	Ethnicity	Mobility Status	Number of Reading Scores	Number of Language Scores	Number of Math Scores
Grade Two	Caucasian	New	7	8	8
	Caucasian	Continuing	4	4	4
	Caucasian	Returning	52	55	55
	Hmong	New	7	7	7
	Hmong	Returning	44	51	51
Grade Three	Caucasian	New	6	6	6
	Caucasian	Continuing	3	2	3
	Caucasian	Returning	56	56	57
	Hispanic	Returning	3	3	3
	Hmong	New	6	6	6
	Hmong	Returning	34	35	36
Grade Four	Caucasian	New	8	8	9
	Caucasian	Continuing	59	69	70
	Caucasian	Returning	9	11	11
	Hmong	Continuing	41	41	41
	Hmong	Returning	1	1	1
Grade Five	Caucasian	New	8	7	8
	Caucasian	Continuing	44	48	48
	Caucasian	Returning	10	12	12
	Hmong	New	3	3	3
	Hmong	Continuing	34	34	34
	Hmong	Returning	2	2	2

In data analyses, clearly show the number of scores represented in an average score, as River Road did in the tables.

SCHOOL **portfolio** RTFOLIO

Easy to use software specifically designed to query student achievement databases is essential for teachers to want to dig deeper into the data in order to understand more about the impact of teaching on student learning.

Examining Matched Scores (Cohort Groups)

Next, we looked at how the students had performed on this standardized test over time. The table shown below, Table 17, shows the data for each category disaggregated by the numbers of years they have taken the tests.

- Years two and three cohorts are students for whom we have test scores for two years
- Years one, two, and three cohorts are students for whom we have test scores for three years

Table 17
Total Reading, Language, and Math NCE Averages and Numbers by Grade Over Time

Grade Level	Cohorts	Total Reading NCE			Total Language NCE			Total Math NCE			Number of Students
		Year 1	Year 2	Year 3	Year 1	Year 2	Year 3	Year 1	Year 2	Year 3	
Grade Three	Years 2, 3 Cohorts		36.7	34.0		41.8	33.8		37.0	37.8	89
Grade Four	Years 2, 3 Cohorts		26.8	29.9		29.4	31.7		28.9	34.0	17
	Years 1, 2, 3 Cohorts	30.5	36.3	37.4	32.8	37.8	41.8	32.7	36.9	45.0	96
Grade Five	Years 2, 3 Cohorts			30.0		28.1	33.9		28.8	40.0	16
	Years 1, 2, 3 Cohorts	32.0	34.4	39.7	32.6	37.3	41.2	32.1	39.8	47.5	86
	Average	31.2	34.8	36.2	32.7	37.8	38.3	32.3	36.9	42.7	Number 304

When we looked at these scores we could see that the students in grades five, four, and two (shown in previous charts) were just about where we expected them to be. In particular, the averages for grades four and five suggested the slow, but steady, progress towards the average that we have worked so hard to achieve.

However, the grade three averages suggested that the students in grade three were doing worse than they had the year before in reading and language. This was definitely not what we expected to see and was very

SCHOOL **portfolio** RTFOLIO

troublesome. The secretary for our district's curriculum director, who is the contact to the test publisher, explored whether we had a problem with the underlying data itself. Since it appears that the data are accurate, we worked to disaggregate the data to see if we could find an answer ourselves.

Digging Deeper into Grade Three Scores

We began by comparing the Total Reading scores because we felt we had spent a lot of effort in that area, and looked at the students by grade and by gender (see Table 18). On the surface, it appeared that we needed to look more closely at our grade three males.

Table 18
Total Reading NCE Averages and Numbers
by Grade and Gender—Years Two and Three

Grade Level	Ethnicity	Total Reading NCE Year 2	Total Reading NCE Year 3	Number of Students
Grade Three	Female	35.1	34.5	49
	Male	38.7	33.3	40
Grade Four	Female	36.7	37.9	61
	Male	32.8	34.4	52
Grade Five	Female	34.9	38.8	52
	Male	31.1	37.5	50
	Average	33.9	35.1	**Number** 384

SCHOOL **portfolio** RTFOLIO

NOTES

When charting student achievement scores over time, be sure to use appropriate equal interval scores.

We disaggregated the averages by looking at just the grade three males and females, by ethnicity (see Figures 18 and 19).

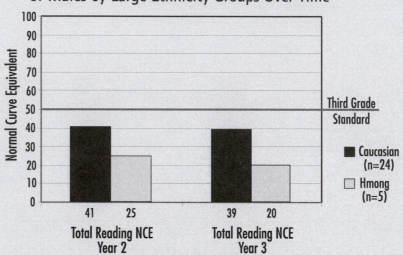

Figure 18
Third Grade Total Reading Score Averages of Males by Large Ethnicity Groups Over Time

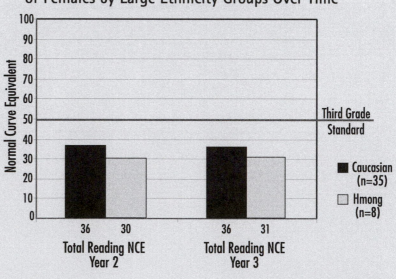

Figure 19
Third Grade Total Reading Score Averages of Females by Large Ethnicity Groups Over Time

SCHOOL portfolio RTFOLIO

NOTES

Normal curve equivalent (NCE) scores were developed to avoid problems that often occur with other types of scores. NCEs are on an equal interval scale and can be aggregated and averaged.

Standard and scaled scores can also be used. However, one needs to watch for maximums on subtests and total tests.

By far, the largest drop was among the five Hmong male students. We then looked at their individual scores to make sure that we didn't have one or two invalid scores that were impacting the average, but that did not appear to be the case.

We wanted to see if English language development (ELD) had anything to do with the averages going down. Looking at all students with scores for one or more of the years, we found that there was a difference between the ELD students and the English-only students in terms of growth in grade three (see Figure 20 and Table 19).

Figure 20
Total Reading NCE Averages Over Time
by Grade and Language Fluency

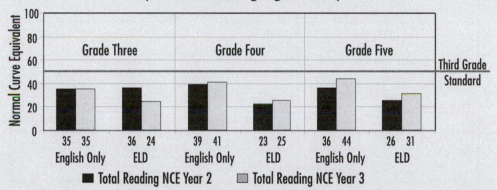

Table 19
Number of Students by Grade
and Language Fluency Over Time

Grade Level	Language Designation	Number of Total Reading NCE Scores Year 2	Number of Total Reading NCE Scores Year 3
Grade Three	English Only ELD	84 19	86 45
Grade Four	English Only ELD	90 47	84 47
Grade Five	English Only ELD	72 46	75 47

SCHOOL **portfolio** PORTFOLIO

When looking at gains, we must follow the same students over time.

The drop in grade three for ELD appeared dramatic, but when we looked at the change in the number of students— from 19 to 45—we realized that we needed to look at cohorts to understand the impact of our programs.

We then took just the grade three scores to see if there was a difference when we disaggregated the data by cohorts of students. From this chart, we learned that the English-only students who had scores for both years had also gone down, although not as dramatically as the ELD student average (see Table 20).

Table 20
Total Reading NCE Averages and Numbers by Cohorts Over Time

Language Designation	Cohorts	Total Reading NCE Year 2	Total Reading NCE Year 3	Number of Reading Scores Year 2	Number of Reading Scores Year 3
English Only	Years 2 & 3 Cohorts	24.9 36.6	36.8 35.1	11 73	13 73
ELD	Years 2 & 3 Cohorts	28.7 37.4	21.7 28.8	3 16	29 16

These are all grade three students.

SCHOOL portfolio RTFOLIO

As Figure 21 shows, we looked at cohorts of ELL students across the school, by grade level and ethnicity, to see how they were doing.

Figure 21
English Language Learner Students
Total Reading NCE Averages by Grade and Ethnicity

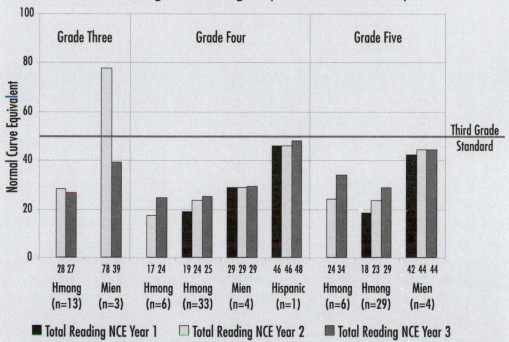

Again, each of these groups shows progress except for grade three. We further disaggregated the averages for ethnic groups by gender, and found that the grade three average for the boys had decreased the most. The girls' average had stayed about the same (see Table 21 on the next page).

SCHOOL portfolio PORTFOLIO

NOTES

Programmatic generalizations cannot be made on the basis of such small Ns. However, we can understand what the students are experiencing with these analyses.

Table 21
ELL Students: Total Reading NCE Averages and Numbers by Grade and Ethnicity

Grade Level	Ethnicity	Gender	Total Reading NCE Year 1	Total Reading NCE Year 2	Total Reading NCE Year 3	Number of Total Reading Scores Year 1	Number of Total Reading Scores Year 2	Number of Total Reading Scores Year 3
Grade Three	Hmong	Female		30.3	30.6		8	8
	Hmong	Male		24.8	19.8		5	5
	Mien	Male		77.7	39.0		3	3
Grade Four	Hmong	Female		22.0	29.0		3	3
	Hmong	Female	22.4	27.2	30.1	19	19	19
	Hmong	Male		12.7	19.7		3	3
	Hmong	Male	14.1	18.4	17.9	14	14	14
	Mien	Female	55.0	52.0	41.0	1	1	1
	Mien	Male	19.7	21.0	25.0	3	3	3
Grade Five	Hispanic	Male	46.0	46.0	48.0	1	1	1
	Hmong	Female		22.0	27.3		3	3
	Hmong	Female	19.3	26.1	28.9	15	15	15
	Hmong	Male		25.7	40.7		3	3
	Hmong	Male	16.6	20.5	27.9	14	14	14
	Mien	Female	33.0	36.0	34.5	2	2	2
	Mien	Male	51.5	52.5	54.0	2	2	2

These are all ELL students, cohorts for at least two years.

We also looked at cohorts by grade level and by language fluency designation, English language learners (ELL), and fluent English proficiency (FEP). Again, all of the students in grades four and five had made progress, but Table 15 also shows a problem with grade three students.

Table 22
ELL Students: Total Reading NCE Averages and Numbers by Grade and Language Fluency—Years One, Two, Three

Grade Level	Language Designation	Total Reading NCE Year 1	Total Reading NCE Year 2	Total Reading NCE Year 3	Number of Total Reading Scores Year 1	Number of Total Reading Scores Year 2	Number of Total Reading Scores Year 3
Grade Three	ELL		23.3	19.7		3	3
	FEP		40.7	30.9		13	13
Grade Four	ELL		11.0	19.8		4	4
	ELL	14.6	18.1	18.4	18	18	18
	FEP		30.0	33.5		2	2
	FEP	25.0	29.7	31.9	19	19	19
Grade Five	ELL	10.6	16.7	22.3	10	10	10
	FEP		24.6	32.6		7	7
	FEP	25.8	30.3	34.1	22	22	22

These are all ELL students, cohorts for at least two years.

SCHOOL 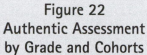 PORTFOLIO

We looked at the grade three authentic assessments to see if the data told a different story, but the data just confirmed that these students were not doing well. Figure 22 below shows the grade three students disaggregated by the same Total Reading cohorts. The students who are cohorts performed better than the students who have not been at the school as long or as much, but neither of the groups met the grade level standards.

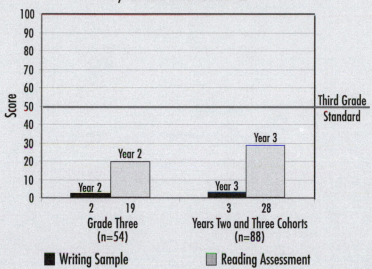

Figure 22
Authentic Assessment
by Grade and Cohorts

SCHOOL PORTFOLIO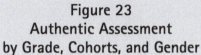

Disaggregating the data by gender showed that the non-cohort girls fared better than the boys, and that there was little difference between the cohort girls and boys (see Figure 23).

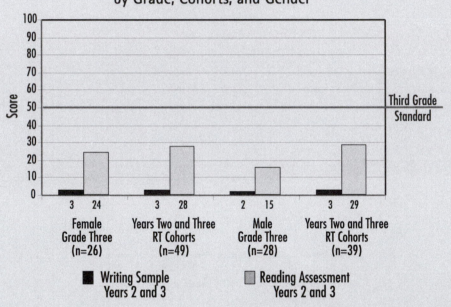

Figure 23
Authentic Assessment
by Grade, Cohorts, and Gender

SCHOOL **portfolio** RTFOLIO

NOTES

Chart whatever student achievement data you have. Your questions will lead you to appropriate next analyses.

Disaggregating the data by ethnicity (groups larger than 10) revealed again that students who have been at the school longer are doing better, and none of the groups have met the grade level standard for these assessments (see Figure 24).

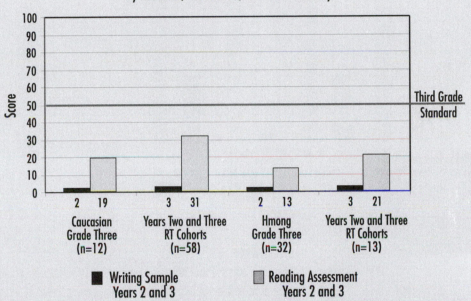

Figure 24
Authentic Assessment
by Grade, Cohorts, and Ethnicity

We also looked at the text-level scores for the grade three students who had participated in the Reading Recovery program in the primary grades. Figure 25 and Table 23 on the next page detail progress for the grade three students in year three, as measured by their text-level scores over three years.

SCHOOL PORTFOLIO

A student achievement database with individual student records is crucial for analyzing data to understand what processes need to change to get different results.

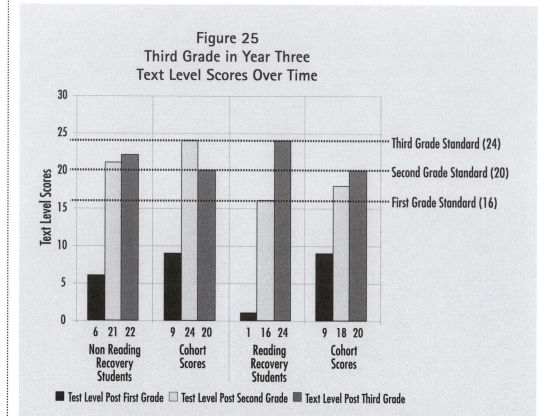

Figure 25
Third Grade in Year Three
Text Level Scores Over Time

Table 23
Third Grade in Years Two and Three
Text Level Scores and Numbers

Grade Three in Years 2 and 3	Text Level Scores				Number of Students				Total Students in Grade 3
	Pre Grade 1	Post Grade 1	Post Grade 2	Post Grade 3	Pre Grade 1	Post Grade 1	Post Grade 2	Post Grade 3	
Non Reading Recovery	0	6	21	22	19	2	86	101	114
Non Reading Recovery Cohorts (Post Scores)	2	9	24	20	8	10	10	10	10
Reading Recovery	-2	1	16	24	1	1	2	1	2
Reading Recovery Cohorts (Post Scores)	-1	9	18	20	23	32	32	32	32
Overall	0	8	20	21	51	45	130	144	158

SCHOOL portfolio RTFOLIO

These results showed us scores at the end of grade three were lower than we would have expected. After all the work in disaggregating grade three data, we came to the following conclusions:

Across the board, the students in grade three were doing even worse than students in the other grades.

- The problem is greater among boys than girls
- The problem is greater among English language learners
- We need to ask ourselves what is different about grade three, since the problem does not seem to be confined to a single group

The discussion of this problem and our plan for resolving it can be found in the Student Achievement section.

Next Steps for Year Four

As you can imagine, there was much discussion about these charts and the story they told at the staff retreat at the beginning of the school year. We are determined to set up a structure that will allow us to prevent another end-of-the-year surprise.

The following changes are planned:

- Alternative assessments will be entered into the database on a regular basis during year four.
- We will have grade level meetings on a quarterly basis to examine our data against the benchmarks we have set for ourselves.
- The principal and the teachers will all have access to the database (with appropriate security) by mid-year so that each of them can bring up student information as they need it. We anticipate being able to send the data to the district at the end of the year.

Ideally, assessments related to the grade level standard are ongoing, so teachers can ensure each student's success, as opposed to finding failures at the end of the year.

Information and Analysis Summary
from the Authors' Perspectives

River Road Progress

Over three years, River Road staff did what they could to get a database established that would help them uncover potential problems via the data, to prevent future student failures, and to make sure all students were achieving. Unfortunately, the district was not there to help River Road get the data they needed. If it had not been for a couple of interested teachers they would not have gotten as far as they did with Information and Analysis. The staff would have continued to do what they had been doing for years and expect different results. With respect to their approach to data collection, this school moved from being reactive—doing only what they had to do for the state and for the district—to being proactive and providing data to help each teacher determine what they could do differently to get different results in the classroom. This staff went from not having a system for data analysis to taking a systematic approach to data. Another significant change was how teachers thought about the children.

Because this staff was paying attention to their data, their scores improved in spite of the fact that their demographics continued to change in ways that might otherwise have resulted in lower scores. Using data helped get the majority of staff committed to continuous improvement. The questionnaires helped them see what needed to change and to hear the voices of the students. The one thing that got the last staff member on board the continuous improvement journey was reading about the Hmong and the Mien people. In understanding about the families' cultures and history, the teachers were able to understand school from the perspective of these students.

Items for the Information and Analysis Section

River Road included some demographic, questionnaire, and student achievement data in their Information and Analysis section. Other things you might consider adding to your Information and Analysis section are:
- Assessments on the Education for the Future Initiative Information and Analysis Continuous Improvement Continuum and discussion about priorities and next steps (River Road's appears in the Continuous Improvement and Evaluation section of their school portfolio)
- Analysis of what needs to happen to move to the next levels in the continuum
- Other demographic data

- Other questionnaire data, such as a questionnaire from perspective employers, former students, middle, and high school staffs
- More information about the school community, district, or school
- More information about all staff and students
- Root cause analyses

Making the Difference for Continuous Improvement

There is no doubt that data make the difference with continuous improvement. Without data, staff can only act on hunches and hypotheses. With data, teachers can understand the results they are getting, based on their processes. With data, teachers can see their progress and strive to make more progress.

Data are important because it helps draw the picture of the school and its community. Data help us understand the needs of our current and future school staff, students, parents, and community. Data point to the root causes of problems so staff do not spin their wheels solving symptoms.

Recommendations

Gathering and analyzing data can be a hook for getting all staff to buy into a continuous improvement process. An online database that every teacher can access and add to is ideal. It is not always possible as staffs begin. A student questionnaire could become an effective catalyst to help staffs see what needs to change. Any effective catalyst will lead staff into wanting additional data.

In putting together this section on Information and Analysis, it is important to get the data in graphic and tabular form as soon as possible. It is the data that can drive the change. Start wherever you can. Questionnaires sometimes pull staff into wanting to look at more data.

The Information and Analysis assessment on the Continuous Improvement Continuums is another way to begin the discussion of what data are needed to continuously improve a school. It is also a good way to determine what to put in this section of the school portfolio. The discussions will begin the process of moving the entire staff in one direction.

Chapter 5
Student Achievement

Introduction to Student Achievement

To fully educate a student, teachers need to do their best during their temporary time together and to care just as much about the educational experiences that the student had before coming and experiences that the student will have after leaving. To believe that the job of a classroom teacher is to operate solely in the present with his or her immediate charge is to deny a school the opportunity to provide a cumulative, purposeful effect.

Carl Glickman

The focus of school improvement is on creating a comprehensive learning organization that understands, cares about, and works for students. In a comprehensive learning organization focused on students, leadership works to prevent student failure as opposed to reactively implementing the latest innovations or taking a fire-fighting approach to making decisions that affect student learning. A focus on students causes leadership to move teachers from roles as providers of information to researchers who understand and can predict the impact of their actions on students and student achievement; and students from recipients of knowledge delivery to goal-setting, self-assessors who produce independent, quality products. In schools where students and student learning are clearly the focus, expected student outcomes are known, teachers collaborate and are skilled in action research, in knowing, predicting, and acting on the impact of their actions to increase student achievement.

Until teachers are able to predict the impact of their actions on students, change their actions based on these predictions, corroborate the effect of their actions with students, and work with peers to build a comprehensive learning organization, any increase in student achievement and change in the classroom will be temporary.

It is often stated in the literature that it takes about five years from the time a school starts to rebuild for increased student achievement to the time it will see sustainable increases in student achievement directly attributable to school improvement efforts. This time can be decreased if the entire school is committed to the school improvement effort and understands the following at the school level and at the individual teacher level:
- Who the school's clients are, and how they learn best
- The impact of current processes on all student learning
- What the school community expects students to know and be able to do

Note. From *The School Portfolio: A Comprehensive Framework for School Improvement,* Second Edition (p.61), by Victoria L. Bernhardt, 1998, Larchmont, NY: Eye on Education. Copyright © 1998 Eye on Education, Inc. Reprinted with permission.

SCHOOL **portfolio** PORTFOLIO

Student Achievement

This Student Achievement section is organized to add new information each year. The current sections are as follows:

Year One	Year Two	Year Three
• Student Expectations	• Vision	• Vision (also referred to in Quality Planning chapter)
• Current Conditions	• Strategies to Increase Student Achievement	
• Strategies to Increase Student Achievement	Literacy/Language Arts	• Strategies to Increase Student Achievement
Literacy/Language Arts	English Language Development	Literacy/Language Arts
English Language Development	Math, Science, and Hands-on Learning	Math, Science, and Hands-on Learning
Math, Science, and Hands-on Learning	• Standards and Assessment	• Standards and Assessment
• Standards and Assessment	Using Student Achievement Data	Student Portfolios
Using Student Achievement Data	• Technology	Using Student Achievement Data
• Student Support Systems	• Student Support Systems	• Technology
• Looking Back on Year One	• Looking Back on Year Two	Impact of Technology
• Next Steps	• Next Steps	• Student Support Systems
		Healthy Start
		Personal and Interpersonal Skills
		• Looking Back on Year Three
		• Next Steps

SCHOOL **portfolio** PORTFOLIO

Student Achievement—Year One

The mission of River Road Elementary School is to provide all students with a positive, secure, and supportive learning environment in which they can acquire the skills and attitudes that foster an enjoyment of learning; respect for themselves and others; and, the physical, emotional, and social competencies necessary to become responsible and productive citizens of the 21st century.

Student Expectations

Several years ago, staff identified the following nine student outcomes, representing skills students need to acquire to be contributing members of society:

- Readiness to learn
- Literacy
- Critical thinking
- Problem-solving skills
- Collaborative skills
- Mastery of mathematics and scientific concepts
- Literacy in technology
- High personal and social efficacy
- An appreciation for lifelong learning

Current Conditions

Despite the hard work of River Road staff, our students have not been as successful academically as we believe they can be. When we looked at our students' standardized test scores, we were struck by how poorly they do across grade levels and gender in all the tests. Overall, the girls seem to score slightly better in language arts and reading than the boys, and there are no noticeable gender differences in math. However, the most obvious pattern is one of low achievement. Staff believe that poor achievement has been caused by several factors:

- Many students lack pre-literacy skills when they enter kindergarten.
- A growing number of River Road's students are immigrants who do not speak English fluently and have had little or no formal education, immediately putting them at a disadvantage.
- In some cases, students come from families that must deal with survival issues and have little time to devote to their children's education.

SCHOOL **portfolio** PORTFOLIO

- The high transiency rate has a negative impact on our students' learning.
- Many students have special needs and do not respond well to traditional school structures and programs.

Retentions have been common in the primary grades. Last year, 14 percent of kindergarten students and 18 percent of students in grade one were retained at the end of the school year. Students were most commonly retained because of poor literacy skills, coupled with developmental indicators that suggested these students needed more time to mature.

Strategies to Increase Student Achievement

Most teachers at River Road try to keep abreast of the latest methods of delivering instruction. Teachers have taken advantage of staff development opportunities that are offered in the district and through a nearby university, in addition to attending conferences. We recognize that students learn in different ways. Teachers are encouraged to try a variety of instructional strategies to address the different learning styles of students. To the degree that time and budget allow, we encourage all staff to be involved in staff development opportunities that will increase student learning.

At each grade level, teachers are encouraged to work together as a team, grouping students for reading skills based on student need. These groupings are flexible. Flexible grouping has been most successful at grade levels where team members have positive and collegial working relationships. River Road does not track students by abilities.

SCHOOL portfolio PORTFOLIO

At first, the approach to improving literacy was primarily to rely on specialists who could only serve a limited number of students. The vision helped teachers take responsibility for developing their skills so that they could serve all students better.

As schools work to improve their student achievement results, teachers must study new instructional approaches.

Literacy/Language Arts

River Road has a strong emphasis on literacy—a theme reflected district-wide. Historically, our students have struggled with attaining literacy at grade level. We have, therefore, adopted the Reading Recovery program which has demonstrated success elsewhere with similar student populations.

We are currently in our third year of using Reading Recovery as an intervention for students experiencing the most difficulty. We have two full-time Reading Recovery teachers to work one-on-one with students who need the most individual help. Figure 26 describes River Road's reading processes.

Last year, River Road piloted literacy group instruction at the second grade level. In the literacy group, a resource teacher used Reading Recovery teaching strategies with small groups of five to six students. The students chosen for literacy group participation were either students who were in the regular classroom, but were not reading at grade level, or students who had already been in the formal Reading Recovery program and were doing better, but were still not reading at grade level.

At the end of last year, the resource and participating classroom teachers felt this strategy had a significant positive impact on the students who had participated in the pilot. Our principal supported the decision both to maintain the grade two literacy groups and to pilot the same strategy  in two of the grade one classrooms this year. The lead resource teacher also expanded her data collection efforts to include the students in the literacy group this year, giving us better information for improving our processes.

SCHOOL **portfolio** RTFOLIO

When teachers document their instruction and assessment processes, they automatically start to improve them. When teachers document their processes, they can see the consistencies and inconsistencies that students feel.

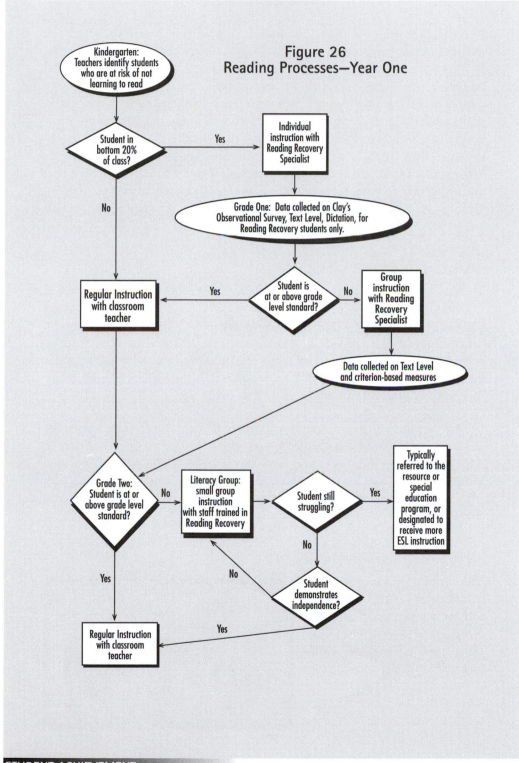

Figure 26
Reading Processes—Year One

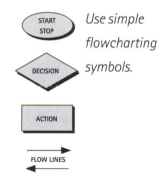

Use simple flowcharting symbols.

START STOP

DECISION

ACTION

FLOW LINES

SCHOOL **portfolio** RTFOLIO

Without a clear schoolwide focus which emerges from concise and repeatable vision/mission statements, professional development is random and sometimes conflicting.

For the first time in years, teachers are observing that students are making better progress in reading. The text level scores of our Reading Recovery students confirm teacher observations. We, therefore, decided to target our Title 1 funding for expansion of the Reading Recovery program. Five additional teachers who teach kindergarten are currently being trained in Reading Recovery which will bring the total number of teachers trained to seven. The kindergarten teachers will teach literacy groups after their own students are dismissed in the afternoon. Informally, the Reading Recovery teachers share strategies with all K-3 staff thereby impacting more students. Several teachers are making serious efforts to implement Reading Recovery strategies for all students

English Language Development

Twenty-six percent of the staff is certified to teach students of limited English proficiency. Teachers serve nearly all students who need support in acquiring English, by using sheltered instruction methods. Since most of our English language learners are Hmong, Hispanic, or Mien, and we have not been able to find teachers who speak their languages, we are not able to consider a bilingual program as an instructional delivery model.

Where possible, instructional assistants have been hired who speak the primary language of our students, and speak and write English fluently. Although these instructional assistants have been helpful to our students, we have not found enough Hmong- and Mien-speaking instructional assistants to serve the growing Southeast Asian population.

Math, Science, and Hands-on Learning

Two years ago, we began to implement the hands-on science program developed at Everystate University. The program involves units that engage students in activities

SCHOOL portfolio PORTFOLIO

Since this school is eligible for Schoolwide Planning under the Improving America's Schools Act (IASA), they created subsections under student achievement, such as "Standards and Assessment", that match the IASA categories. In fact, all systemic change processes address the same necessary data. With the creative use of sub-dividers and cross references, the school portfolio can be used for multiple requirements.

such as constructing and using pulleys, observing and measuring shadows, and experimenting with the surface tension of water. An important element of the program is having students record and discuss their observations. One teacher at each grade level has been trained in this program. It is that teacher's responsibility to provide information and materials at grade-level meetings. Although we have been using many of the grade-level meetings this year to work on hands-on science implementation, we are aware that implementation is still spotty.

Two grade three teachers attended Adopt-A-Watershed (AAW) training this year have begun to implement the AAW curriculum units together. Students have learned about seed dispersal of native and non-native plants through observations along the river that runs near our school. These units are a good match to the hands-on science program.

In math, the district is considering adopting a new textbook emphasizing hands-on learning. One of our teachers has taken an active role in the selection committee. Assuming that the adoption goes forward, teachers will be trained by the district next year in hands-on math, using the textbook more like a resource than as a traditional text.

Standards and Assessment

At the district level, we are beginning to move in the direction of a standards-based assessment system. Some River Road teachers serve on the district language arts standards committee that will complete language arts standards by the end of the year. At this point, only a few of our staff members have a clear vision of how a standards-based assessment system would work in practice.

Currently, assessment practices at our school vary widely. Some teachers rely heavily on traditional grading systems, especially at the upper grades. Others use a mix of authentic assessment and traditional grading. At the primary level, a few teachers have begun to use portfolios with their students, and we have encouraged all teachers to move in that direction. This year, we spent quite a bit of time discussing how student portfolios would be used in conjunction with the new language arts standards.

SCHOOL portfolio PORTFOLIO

NOTES

Once schools begin to use data to inform practice, they generally discover the need for a database that is accessible at the site and preferably on the teachers' desks.

Using Student Achievement Data

This is the first year that we have systemically tried to use data to inform our decisions about the instructional program. Our first attempts have led us to the realization that while we have quite a lot of data, it is not organized in a way that allows us to use it well.

For example:

- Most of our data are on paper records and not in a database, allowing us to disaggregate by program, ethnicity, and/or gender. Teachers receive their test data in the fall for the previous year. We can not organize historical data by the new class assignments and, therefore, the data are not very helpful in improving instruction.
- Due to the way in which we kept student records in the past, we cannot go back and look at historical data for the same students unless we go through student files, one-by-one.
- We believe that norm-referenced tests do not tell the full story, but we have no standardized alternative assessments that can be reported schoolwide.

Student Support Systems

Recognizing that some students need support beyond that available in the classroom, River Road has worked with the district to provide a variety of special services.

- We have two full-time resource teachers to work with students with learning disabilities. These teachers work primarily in collaboration with classroom teachers, and sometimes pull out students to work on skills. We also have a self-contained special day class.

- When a teacher believes that a student has special needs that require attention, the student is referred to the Student Study

SCHOOL **portfolio** PORTFOLIO

Team. The purpose of the team is to try to match student needs with resources that are available through the school, district, or community.

- We are committed to make every effort to place students with limited English proficiency in classrooms with teachers who are certified to teach them.

- We are in the exploratory stage of applying for a Healthy Start grant with social service and health agencies in our community. Both the Parks and Recreation Department and the YMCA have agreed to offer extended day programs here next year, whether or not we obtain the grant. (See the Partnership Development section of this portfolio.)

Looking Back on Year One

As we reflect on the work we have done over the past few years, we see that there are many pockets of excellent work. However, by encouraging teachers to choose their own professional development, we inadvertently set up rivalries for scarce resources between programs advocated by different teachers. We need to get clearer on where we are going and use standards and assessment as a way to understand and improve our progress.

YEAR ONE

SCHOOL portfolio TFOLIO

Self-assessing on the Continuous Improvement Continuums and writing next steps helps focus staff for the next year on what they need to do to improve.

Next Steps

- *Vision*—We need a vision that is developed and shared by our school community and a single plan to implement the vision. As we worked on our portfolio this year, we realized that the mission and student expectations we have mean different things to different people, and we have no real vision. We need to be absolutely clear about where we are going, and how we are going to get there.

- *Standards and Assessment*—We need to be clear on what we want our students to know and be able to do. To that end, we will participate fully in district committees that are charged with developing standards. We also need to develop a few good alternative assessments and rubrics for assessment that can be used in addition to norm-referenced tests.

- *Use of Data*—We need to develop a better data collection system so that we can use data for decision-making in order to improve student achievement.

- *Programs/strategies*—We can see that we are working in too many different directions. We need to focus our work more. Until we have a vision of where we are going, it will be hard to become more focused.

- *Student Services*—What we are not doing is clear when we review the list of what we are doing. We are not taking advantage of our own community to help us provide services to students. We need to investigate parent and community partnerships further.

SCHOOL **portfolio** RTFOLIO

Student Achievement — Year Two

Vision

Just before school began in the fall, many active parents and almost the entire staff held a retreat to create a vision that would drive our work and focus our attention around how we will increase student achievement and success in our school. This vision has, in fact, driven our work this year. (See Quality Planning for details.) We spent much of the fall researching best practices that would be consistent with attaining our vision for student achievement. From this, we developed a single school plan and began to make the many changes in our programs and instructional strategies that will get us to our vision for students. Our work to improve student achievement over the next years will be focused on the following four goals:

- Literacy by grade three
- Curriculum and assessment based on standards
- Integrating technology into the curriculum
- Using hands-on, project-based instruction

Strategies to Increase Student Achievement

We continue to receive students who lack pre-literacy skills. However, the awareness of the staff about how to serve students' needs has increased through the work of our study teams. Furthermore, for the first time, we are beginning to use data in ways that further our understanding of the impact of our processes on students. We have focused our energy more this year on using content areas to build literacy through hands-on learning, and on tackling our students' low achievement in reading through expanding Reading Recovery. At the same time, we have been working all year on district committees developing content and performance standards in language arts and math.

NOTES

There needs to be one vision for the school, therefore, if the vision is mentioned in student achievement, there is no other vision anywhere else in the school portfolio. This vision can be mentioned again, but it is the same vision.

SCHOOL portfolio PORTFOLIO

If instructional strategies are not a part of the vision, they become add-ons that are only implemented unevenly.

Literacy/Language Arts

This year, kindergarten teachers who had been trained in Reading Recovery techniques began providing additional literacy groups so that we could serve more students. This was possible because the kindergarten program is shorter than the grades one through three school day. Figure 27 shows our process interventions in reading.

In addition to these Reading Recovery teachers, the classroom teachers who had been trained are now beginning to use Reading Recovery strategies in their regular instruction. The literacy groups are still the responsibility of the resource teachers, but more literacy groups were offered as a result of the increased resource staff. We now provide literacy groups for all students reading below grade level in kindergarten through grade two, except those receiving individual instruction through Reading Recovery (bottom 20 percent of readers).

Text -level data collected from the last two years reinforce our belief that this process is really making a difference with the students. However, too many of our students are still reading below grade-level standards. We need to begin using Reading Recovery strategies sooner with more students and make sure all K-3 teachers know how to use Reading Recovery strategies in their classrooms.

English Language Development

We continue to stress the importance of teachers receiving their language development certification and using sheltered instruction techniques in their classrooms. Although several additional teachers received their certification this year, we are just keeping up with the increase in our English language learning population. Several teachers who teach using these techniques believe that the techniques would benefit many of our native English speakers who have poor oral language skills. They have been encouraged to share the techniques with others during grade-level meetings.

SCHOOL **portfolio** PORTFOLIO

When teachers begin to clarify their processes, they begin to see the impact of their actions on students. In other words, they can see the effects of what they are doing by the results they are getting.

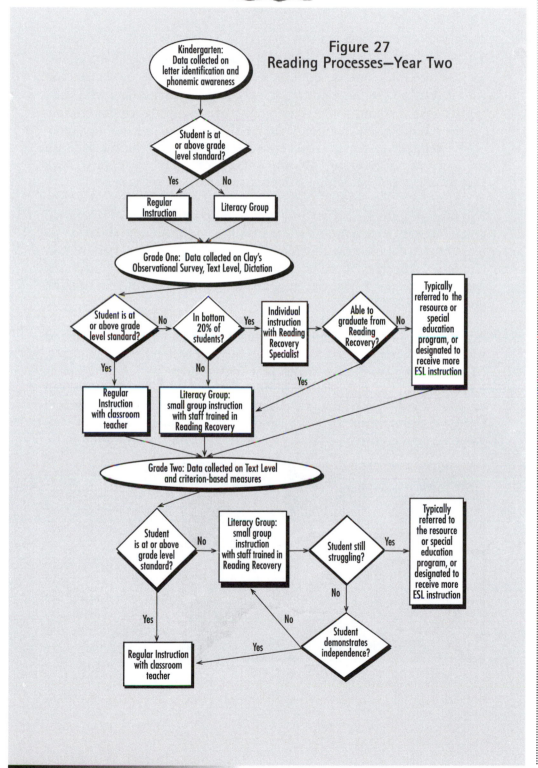

Figure 27
Reading Processes—Year Two

SCHOOL portfolio RTFOLIO

*Data clarifies the problems.
The staff then need to
develop the skills to
implement solutions
within the context of
the vision/mission.*

Math, Science, and Hands-on Learning

This year, we entered into partnerships with several local resources, such as the University Agricultural Extension, to help us implement the Adopt-A-Watershed curriculum more broadly. Two teachers who were trained last year and several community members advocated strongly for the school's participation. Although the program ties well to hands-on learning, some teachers feel that there is not enough time to teach the current curriculum, let alone take on new programs. This partnership will begin with voluntary participation by teachers.

Not all staff participated in the districtwide training on hands-on math. Some teachers have continued to teach basic mathematics skills, while beginning to implement the new program. While we are believers in hands-on learning, there is some concern among the faculty that students need to memorize math facts as well as understand the underlying concepts.

Since hands-on math training was a district requirement, we wanted to use it toward our goal of integrated instruction with a focus on literacy. Math journals were the obvious first step. Students in all classrooms began to write math journals this year as a way for them to both reflect on their problem-solving in math and increase their skills in analytical thinking and writing. Twice, we asked all students to write about the value of their journals. This provided us with some useful data.

Teachers feel that math journals have been very successful, and student reaction has been very positive.

We have also found several ways to connect the math units to the hands-on science units that some teachers were already using, but the connections are not nearly as strong as we want them to be. As we try to integrate instruction, we keep coming back to the question: What

SCHOOL portfolio TFOLIO

do we want students to know and be able to do? We recognize that we are still at the beginning of a long journey, but at least we know where we are headed.

Standards and Assessment

While some of our staff have been serving on district standards committees, we have moved forward with the development of school-level language arts assessments. We do not view this as contradictory work; rather, we see ourselves as leaders in the district and believe that working on both fronts will get us to our goal faster. Interestingly, the other members of the district language arts standards committee also see us as leaders.

Early in the fall, staff created and began to pilot a six-step writing rubric to complement district standards in language arts. In May, that rubric (see Figure 28) was adopted by the district for use with the new writing assessment.

Now, with the year nearly at a close, we have—
- district language arts content standards in place
- piloted several language arts assessments by different teachers
- developed a writing assessment, using our six-point rubric, to be implemented districtwide next year
- two reading assessments (one K-3 and one 4-5) to be implemented districtwide next year
- district math standards that are near completion

The district assessments in language arts are performance based, in line with the River Road vision. We feel that we have come a long way since last year, both schoolwide and districtwide, yet this practice is still very new to us. We recognize that connecting standards and performance-based assessments to teaching and learning will take several years of hard work.

In reading, we continue to use the text-level scoring to regularly assess students' abilities and needs. Most of our teachers now have the skills to assess students accurately, using the text levels.

We spent quite a bit of time talking about student portfolios this year. Conceptually, teachers agree that student portfolios help students understand what they know and are able to do, and help students be a part of their own assessment and improvement.

SCHOOL PORTFOLIO

Figure 28
River Road Elementary School Writing Rubric

Level 6	Level 5	Level 4
Student work— • consistently pursues a strong, central purpose across a complex range of ideas • skillfully engages the reader and shows exceptional insight into the subject • includes main ideas that are developed comprehensively and supported with a variety of logical reasons and detailed examples • is skillfully organized • shows distinctive style through skillful and expressive use of vocabulary, phrasing, and sentence structure • demonstrates essentially error-free control of grammar, punctuation, capitalization, and spelling	Student work— • consistently pursues a central purpose, holds the interest of the reader, and shows insight into the subject • includes main ideas that are developed and supported by a variety of reasons and examples • is effectively organized • shows emerging style through effective use of vocabulary, phrasing, and sentence structure • consistently demonstrates the accurate use of grammar, punctuation, capitalization, and spelling	Student work— • shows a consistent purpose, communicates to the reader, and connects the writer's knowledge to the subject • includes main ideas that are organized, developed, and supported by reasons and examples • shows suitable vocabulary, phrasing, and sentence structure • generally demonstrates the accurate use of grammar, punctuation, capitalization, and spelling
Level 3	Level 2	Level 1
Student work— • shows a purpose, but may be inconsistent in communicating to the reader or connecting the writer's knowledge to the subject • includes main ideas that may be organized or partially developed and supported by some reasons and examples • may show imprecise use of vocabulary, phrasing, and sentence structure • includes some errors in the use of grammar, punctuation, capitalization, and spelling	Student work— • attempts to connect the writer's knowledge to the subject and may not show a pupose • is typically brief, unorganized, and underdeveloped • may include frequent errors in the use of grammar, capitalization, punctuation, and spelling	Student work— • is too brief or disorganized to communicate to the reader • may not connect the writer's knowledge to the subject • typically includes many errors in the use of grammar, capitalization, punctuation, and spelling

SCHOOL *portfolio* RTFOLIO

NOTES

Peer coaching is one of the most effective and supportive ways to get teachers truly implementing new approaches in their classrooms.

Grade-level discussions at teachers' meetings on "what works well" can focus on effective classroom practices.

We have continued to increase our use of student portfolios this year. About 50 percent of the teachers have begun using student portfolios, but, in many classrooms, these portfolios are really more like scrapbooks of students' work. We need to connect the portfolios to standards, using rubrics for assessment, and using anchor papers to make scoring consistent. Our performance standards are not adequately in place to use portfolios as successfully as we would like.

Using Student Achievement Data

Although we became more conscious about using data this year, we are just now getting to the point where we have a database that could be used for action research. Earlier this year, we looked at the norm referenced test reports from the test publisher and began to systematically keep our own data about students' text-level reading scores. At the end of the year, we compared the percent of grade three students meeting grade-level standards using text-level scores and CTBS scores. We used grade three because research shows that this is the point at which students must be readers if they are to be successful in school.

Text level scores seem to be increasing, but we have not yet done the level of analysis that allows us to look at matched scores by gender, ethnic group, program, and grade level. Nevertheless, we are heartened to see that at grade three more students are meeting the grade-level benchmark based on their text-level scores. However, CTBS test data showed a drop in the same year, which we believe reflects the new state mandate requiring all English language learners who have been residents for one year to be tested in English. Over the summer, several of the teachers on the leadership team and our schoolwide plan coordinator (we no longer call her the Title 1 coordinator) are planning to learn to use the database to test such hypotheses.

Although our use of data is still very basic, we see that we worked very hard this year to get a plan into place to address student achievement, we are only at the very beginning of the implementation process. We need to implement our plans much more before we can expect to see substantial changes in student achievement.

SCHOOL portfolio PORTFOLIO

NOTES

When schools are clear on what they expect students to know and be able to do, it is then sensible to think about how technology can support the achievement of those skills.

Technology

Although we agreed in our vision that technology will be a tool to improve student achievement, our plan dictated use of much of our professional development time and dollars to developing standards, hands-on math, and literacy. We have had many discussions of how technology can be used as a tool in the classroom, but we have only a few teachers who have the skills themselves to use technology as a tool. We,

therefore, wrote a technology specialist (paraprofessional) position into our plan. The technology specialist's role is to—

- assist teachers in increasing their ability to integrate technology
- develop a "Tech Wizards" program for students in grades four and five who want to help teachers and become mentors to younger children
- support the use of e-mail buddies to increase student writing skills
- move forward with the implementation of the technology plan (part of our school plan)

For technology, our idea was to use a "Collaborative Model" designed after our Special Education Resource Program. We broke up one of our two computer labs and put the computers on mobile carts. The technology specialist and classroom teachers plan activities together that are integrated into the curriculum. As the technology specialist works side-by-side with teachers, the teachers gain technology skills and the specialist gains teaching skills. In filling the position, we were fortunate to find a recent college graduate with technology skills who wants to become a credentialed

SCHOOL portfolio RTFOLIO

Schools that are conscientious about improving classroom-level processes and school-level processes simultaneously are more able to move quickly toward their vision.

technology teacher in the future. The specialist brings a mini-lab to the classrooms, as needed (up to six computers depending upon need). We view these rolling labs as temporary until we can build a set of 4-6 networked computers in each classroom.

Although we expected to have a network in place this year, completion fell behind schedule and is now anticipated by next fall. Through the network, teachers will be able to access the Internet and send electronic mail messages to each other to improve communication. Students will also be able to use the Internet and e-mail as part of the instructional program.

Student Support Systems

Last year, as we looked at the student support services we had in place, we recognized that we needed to make better use of community resources in order to serve students.

As the parent and community involvement committee was exploring the possibility of applying for a Healthy Start Grant, it became clear that we could provide the following after-school programs this year, with or without the grant:

- The Parks and Recreation Department has begun an after-school sports program using our outside school space and cafeteria. While it is open to all children in the city, it will primarily serve our students.
- The YMCA began an after-school daycare program for K-3 students mid-year. The after-school program shares the kindergarten rooms, which has been difficult for some teachers, but overall there is support for the program by both staff and the community.

We also did proceed with the Healthy Start grant application, which was submitted this spring. We are awaiting notification by the end of June. (See Chapter 9, Partnership Development.)

SCHOOL **portfolio** PORTFOLIO

Looking Back on Year Two

This has been a highly productive year! We have a clear path for increasing student achievement laid out before us. We have content and performance standards in place in language arts, and content standards in place in math. We have added additional support in reading for low-achieving students, broadened hands-on learning in the classrooms, and created

partnerships with local agencies to support student and family needs. We have also learned to study our student achievement results along with our school processes.

Next Steps

We are at the point where our work is quite focused and there is broad buy-in to our vision. Our goal is to implement the vision throughout the school and in every classroom. To accomplish this, next year we plan to—

- examine student assessment data regularly, as a whole faculty and in grade-level teams
- become more involved in action research in our individual classrooms
- use technology more to support learning
- develop a non-threatening process for peer coaching
- continue to find or develop integrated thematic units that use technology to support literacy
- share our work, so that every child in the school can benefit from each teacher's talents
- enter the authentic assessment data we are collecting individually into the database, so we can use it for action research

SCHOOL portfolio RTFOLIO

Student Achievement — Year Three

Vision

It is now hard to believe that three years ago teachers were pursuing their own path to school improvement and, as a school, we were unfocused. We are now very clear about where we are going and the path we need to follow to get there. What has changed most in the last year is our understanding of the importance of long-term planning. At first, we wanted to do everything immediately. As a result, we worked very hard, accomplished a great deal, but did not nearly get through what we had planned. This was very demoralizing. Although the ink was barely dry on our multi-year school action plan, we recognized that we had to revise it to set more realistic timelines that still push all of us to work hard, but are achievable. We want to give ourselves the time to work deeply and make the changes stick. The most exciting part of our work is that we can now see the impact on student achievement. This change, together with a maintainable pace, is keeping everyone working toward the vision.

Strategies to Increase Student Achievement

There was a very noticeable increase in implementation of our vision at the classroom level this year. Parents and district office administrators often commented that children were involved in more hands-on activities and seemed to be more focused on their work than in the past.

Literacy/Language Arts

This year, we asked the district speech therapist to help us screen the kindergarten students who were not performing at grade level by mid-year. We improved our process for assigning students to literacy groups so that all students who are below grade level get support, either through Reading Recovery (one-on-one), literacy groups, or through Reading Recovery strategies implemented by the classroom teacher. These processes are shown in Figure 29. All of the K-3 classroom teachers have been trained and either have been using or are beginning to use Reading Recovery strategies in their classroom.

YEAR THREE

SCHOOL portfolio PORTFOLIO

Note how different Figure 29 looks from Figures 26 and 27. River Road teachers examined their data and changed their processes.

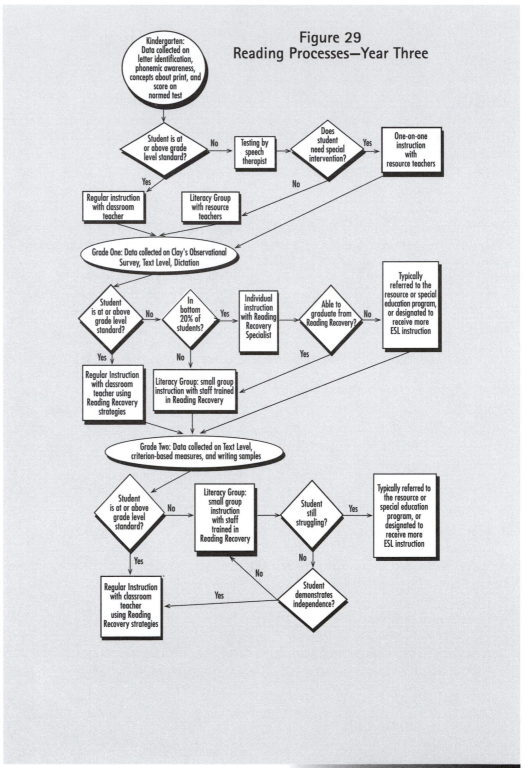

Figure 29
Reading Processes—Year Three

SCHOOL **portfolio** RTFOLIO

Math, Science, and Hands-on Learning

Adopt-A-Watershed is becoming a significant way to provide hands-on instruction, while giving students meaningful service learning experiences. Last year, four teachers were trained and participated. Students and parents were so enthusiastic that, this year, seven additional teachers chose to be trained onsite to begin participating with their students.

The degree to which instruction is project-based still varies considerably from classroom to classroom, but there is a definite move in the right direction. The culture of our school now encourages sharing much more than in the past. Teachers who are in the forefront of developing projects provide their units to other teachers in their grade level.

For example, one of the grade five teachers began a project in which students, working in teams, built motorized vehicles using Legos and controlled them by computer using Logo, a simple programming language. The project was a simulation of moving boulders for a construction project and required students to develop knowledge in both math and science. Students kept written and photographic journals of what they had observed and created a presentation in Hyperstudio at the end of the unit. Two other teachers have asked for support next year in using this project.

NOTES

Without a clear schoolwide focus, professional development is random and sometimes conflicting.

A performance assessment can be built into student work so that they become two sides of the same coin. Teachers then use these assessments to improve teaching on an ongoing basis.

Whether performance expectations are academic or personal/behaviorial, consistency throughout the school makes a big difference in student success.

Standards and Assessment

We now have both language arts and math assessments in place districtwide that have been aligned with the newly adopted district standards. We have begun to use the standards to build the curriculum, using projects in many of the classrooms. We have developed several schoolwide assessments in reading, writing, and math. We also are embedding problem-solving assessments into project-based units as we develop them.

The outcome of all this work is that data are showing that student achievement is improving gradually, but consistently, when we look at students who have remained in our school. The improvement shows in both authentic measures and in the state-mandated tests.

Student Portfolios

Student portfolios are a much more common feature in classrooms than they were two years ago when we began to track our progress. The portfolios include writing samples, student multimedia presentations, photographs of students' projects, and students' reflections on their work. Beginning in grade three, students assist the teacher in deciding how well they are meeting the standards and what work will be included in the portfolio. Students are more aware of performing quality work through the use of scoring rubrics. Self-assessment also gives students more ownership of their learning.

Samples of math work are collected in connection with our standards, but we have not yet anchored the assessments as effectively as we did in language arts. We need to work as a group to improve inter-rater reliability, especially in math, so every teacher's assessment of the same student work would be identical.

SCHOOL **portfolio** PORTFOLIO

NOTES

If data are not being used, hunches and hypotheses about why certain results are occurring may result in wrong actions being taken.

Using Student Achievement Data

River Road began to collect program level data for all K-3 students. Specifically, data were collected from kindergarten students at mid-year and at the end of the year, and from all students in grades one, two, and three at the beginning and end of the year. Students in Reading Recovery and literacy groups were also tested mid-year. To determine if the process was having a sustainable result with students, the lead resource teacher also worked with teachers in grades four and five to ensure that text levels were assessed at those grades as well.

This year, we finally had the database in place that allowed us to look at different subgroups of students and see if our efforts are impacting achievement. Once we were able to disaggregate student achievement and look at matched scores within subgroups over time, we discovered that most groups had experienced more than a year's growth in standardized test scores in math, language arts, and reading. (Actual data is found in the Information and Analysis section of this portfolio.) Text-level scores are also increasing at a rate greater than one year's growth. This was very rewarding, with one exception. First, we noticed that grade three reading scores and language arts scores did not seem to show the improvement that the math scores showed. Since there is so much mobility at our school, we looked at matched scores to see whether grade three students who were with us last year showed growth. Much to our surprise and dismay, we found that there was actually a decrease in scores. When we disaggregated the matched scores, we discovered that most of the decrease was among our English language learners.

It was hard for everyone to look at this discovery from a perspective of problem-solving and not blame. Our first reaction was to blame the testing company. Once we established that they had not made an error, we needed to look closely at ourselves. This discovery truly tested the trust and collaboration we had worked so hard to create among the staff. There are many very young, energetic, committed grade three teachers who were questioning their own competency upon seeing the data. In looking closer, we had to ask ourselves how we, as a school, had allowed so many new teachers to be concentrated in grade three, and why we had not extended Reading Recovery literacy groups to that grade.

Once we asked the right questions, the answers were obvious. Several years ago, the state legislature lowered class size substantially in three primary grades. School districts could choose grades K-2 or grades 1-3; ours chose grades K-2 for lower class sizes. At that time, most of the grade three teachers moved into grades one or two so they could have smaller classes, and new teachers were hired at the grade three level. We assumed that it was in the interest of beginning readers to have the more experienced teachers early in the process. At about the same time, we began Reading Recovery, logically targeting the early grades. We did not see that we had essentially left a whole team of new teachers on their own to develop their skills in teaching reading and language arts. Although they had the same collaborative time as other teachers, they did not have the support of expert teachers at the grade three level to coach them in their professional development. All of the teachers who were trained in Reading Recovery were concentrated in the K-2 classes.

In reflecting upon the data, we realized that we were operating on the assumption that grade three was less crucial than the earlier years and that we did not need to concentrate as much attention on instruction at that grade level. Not only had we put our least experienced teachers there, but we had not supported grade three students with additional Reading Recovery literacy groups.

We therefore need to adjust our plans for next year by continuing literacy groups into grade three. This will be achieved by training the grade three team and the three kindergarten teachers not already trained. One of our experienced Reading Recovery teachers has offered to go back to a grade three class next year and mentor the grade three team.

Our test data shows that our math scores are higher and have increased more than our reading scores. After we finished congratulating ourselves on improving math instruction, we asked how well we are using hands-on math and science experiences for writing and reading

SCHOOL portfolio RTFOLIO

NOTES

When teachers begin to clarify their processes, they begin to see the impact of their actions on students. In other words, they can see the effects of what they are doing by the results they are getting.

across the curriculum. Teachers collected sample writings in math and science to examine together from the point of view of the language arts standards. Again, we made an important discovery. We were writing across the curriculum, but we were not holding students to the same high standards for their writing in math and science as we were for their writing in language arts! Several teachers commented that as long as students were demonstrating understanding in the math or science content, they did not feel that they had time to ask students to revise their writing to meet language arts standards. We still have a way to go to truly integrate instruction using a project-based approach.

Technology

The good news is that we now are connected to the district network in the main building and through most classrooms. The bad news is that the network does not yet extend to the portable classrooms that were added to accommodate class size reduction. Therefore, e-mail has only transformed the way some teachers and students communicate and learn. The additional networking is expected to be in place by the fall.

Our emphasis has been on using technology to support literacy through hands-on learning. Our goal is to have students regularly document their work on projects using technology. Currently, about two-thirds of the staff regularly use computers for instruction in some way. In many classes, students are involved in projects that give them a real reason to read and write. Using Hyperstudio, all of the students in grades four and five now create at least one multimedia presentation of their work each year. At the primary level, children in several classes now have adult e-mail buddies. Teachers have found that regular correspondence with a caring adult leads children to work very hard to read and write. Our technology specialist has been instrumental in integrating technology by working in the classrooms along with the classroom teachers.

Despite our commitment to use technology to increase student achievement, the general level of expertise on the staff is uneven. Now that we are further along on standards and assessment, we can begin to put more staff time into developing skills in using technology across the curriculum.

SCHOOL portfolio PORTFOLIO

NOTES

Research studies indicate that students write more and write more fluently when they write using word processing.

Taking a systems approach to schoolwide improvement leads to looking beyond the school. The school is the logical "community center" for an integrated approach to serving the needs of students and their families.

Impact of Technology

In classes where students use technology more, teachers have observed that students are more willing to write and edit their work when they use computers. The technology specialist recently provided us with several articles that corroborate this observation. This information has turned many teachers' minds about technology, giving them an incentive to learn to use technology more as part of the curriculum.

Many teachers have also taken advantage of technology to improve their own effectiveness. Some keep records with computers, such as the minutes for shared decision-making meetings, while others have produced professional-looking documents and classroom materials.

In the two grade one classrooms that had adult e-mail buddies this year, students far exceeded the literacy standards. Teachers and parents felt that this use of technology had really paid off for students; therefore, the grade two teachers are now willing to continue the work begun in grade one.

Our Tech Wizards have had a wonderful impact on the school, providing the scaffolding for young children to use technology (and for some teachers, too). Several of the Tech Wizards are students who have difficulty with reading and writing. Through technology, these students found an area in which they excel and can contribute to their school community.

Student Support Systems

In addition to continuing previous services, we added a grandparent reading program this year which has benefited many of our beginning readers, especially those who are experiencing difficulty in reading. (See Partnership Development section of this portfolio.) The biggest change for us, however, was Healthy Start.

Healthy Start

Last year, when several faculty members, social service agencies, health agencies, and community members began writing for a Healthy Start

SCHOOL portfolio RTFOLIO

grant, others supported it, but did not really understand fully the impact it would have. At that time, we explored ways to integrate health services onsite in order to serve the many children who have inadequate health services. Much to our delight, we were awarded the grant. We had never before won a grant of this magnitude. We now have an onsite children's health clinic that also provides health education for parents and family counseling services. (See Partnership Development.)

The impact has been a dramatic increase in the number of parents who are in the school. It is not at all unusual now for parents to drop into class with their toddlers in tow to observe an older child, while waiting for clinic appointments. Many teachers found this difficult at first, but, overall, we know that the benefits outweigh the disadvantages.

Personal and Interpersonal Skills

Our work this year on increasing hands-on learning meant that more children were working in groups. As we observed our students working, we could see that their lack of interpersonal skills was getting in the way of their ability to learn. In the past, teachers used a variety of programs to help students improve their personal and social skills. Since all of these were used to focus on inter- and intrapersonal skills, we asked staff to come to consensus on the core values, skills, and vocabulary that we would use (such as confidence, perseverance, and trust). Once consensus was reached, everyone on staff agreed to reinforce these skills throughout the curriculum in an effort to enhance students' personal habits and augment their collaborative skills. By setting consistent behavioral expectations, and using the same terms, we are finding that students are more likely to meet these expectations.

YEAR THREE

SCHOOL portfolio PORTFOLIO

Looking Back on Year Three

This year, we became far more proficient in using data for improvement. Teachers began to use the database much more at the classroom level and, by the end of the year, saw the need to enter ongoing assessment data for their own use.

In the classrooms, instructional strategies and processes are beginning to come together so that all students experience a high quality program that is in line with standards and uses hands-on methods, rich in the use of technology. Peer coaching has had a major effect in making this possible.

Next Steps

- *Standards and Assessment*—We need to improve inter-rater reliability, especially in math, by establishing anchor papers and training all staff in using them.

- *Use of Data*—We need to increase the use of data, at all levels, into our routines. This has become a common process, but needs to become habitual.

- *Programs/Strategies*—We need to expand peer coaching, and look for ways for teachers to work together more so that our best practices become our most common practices.

- *Technology*—We need to emphasize supporting learning with telecommunications, once the network is fully in place.

Student Achievement Summary from the Authors' Perspectives

River Road Progress

River Road staff worked very hard with respect to student achievement over the past three years. The staff developed a vision that was shared. They became clear on their purpose and they will be clear on what they expect students to know and be able to do, with the help of the district standards and assessments committee. As these teachers were able to gather, analyze, and utilize data with respect to their processes, they could see the impact of their actions on student learning. Teachers were able to see where new strategies were needed and which students needed additional support. Staff professional development focused on improving teaching and learning in ways that met their students' needs. This staff did a good job of balancing district requirements with their own work. Instead of waiting until the district standards and assessments committee work was complete and mandated, they moved forward with the development of school level standards, tied to assessments, and factored these into their database design.

It is obvious that none of the progress the teachers made with respect to student achievement could have been made without the use of data. When River Road teachers used data while looking at their processes, they started to see what needed to change to get different results with their students.

Items for the Student Achievement Section

Items that might go in this Student Achievement section of your school portfolio include the following:

- Assessments on the Education for the Future Initiative Student Achievement Continuous Improvement Continuum and discussion about priorities and next steps (River Road's appears in the Continuous Improvement and Evaluation section of their school portfolio)
- Description of current instructional and assessement strategies
- Standardized test scores, over time, by subgroup (i.e., ethnic, gender, language proficiency, socioeconomic status, how long they have been at the school, comparisons to the district, state, other schools, if appropriate) (Might also appear in Information and Analysis)
- Other measures of student learning, over time, by subgroup (e.g., performance assessment scores, local measures)
- Analyses of the results of different assessment strategies
- Instructional implications of the school's student population

- Gaps in learning/analysis of student learning needs
- Essential student learnings/standards and how they were determined
- Description of instructional and assessment strategies desired to implement to meet student learning needs
- Reasons teachers know these strategies will meet the needs of the students and prevent student failure
- Plan for implementation
- Description of strategy to support implementation (e.g., action research, rubrics, peer coaching) (Might also appear in Professional Development)
- Evaluation of implementation and impact of strategies
- Exhibits of quality student work
- Analyses of what needs to happen to move up in the Student Achievement Continuum (Might appear in Continuous Improvement and Evaluation)
- Goals for improvement

Making the Difference for Continuous Improvement

It is clear that until schools know their students, and have determined what they expect students to know and be able to do, there is no way that comprehensive and consistent changes will take place throughout the school. Once standards or essential student learnings are identified, teachers are able to build a continuum of learning that makes sense for students and, therefore integrate technology, curriculum, and assessments. Identifying what schools expect students to know and be able to do requires clarity of a vision for the school. Visions that will be shared ultimately must be built on the values and beliefs of the school community and a clear purpose. A shared vision is one that all will understand, and implement, in the same way. A shared vision can focus schoolwide attention and help alleviate too much on their plate.

Probably the most crucial element in the puzzle of creating student achievement increases is teachers' understandings of their processes documented in relationship to the results they are getting. When teachers can see the impact of their actions on the students they are teaching, they will never work again without data and documentation. With this combination, every teacher can be sure that every student is achieving, and if not, what they need to do to change to get different results.

Recommendations

Every school can get the results River Road teachers got, even better—and faster, if they start with data and a shared vision. It took River Road three years to get set up, in one sense. We recommend that schools and districts commit their resources to getting a quality student achievement database in place so teachers can conduct action research, measure the impact of their processes against the results, and figure out how to work differently to get different results. With such a database in place, the solutions to student achievement increases will begin to emerge.

Additionally important is a vision that is truly shared by all members of the school community. This vision needs to be built on the values and beliefs of the individuals, and the purpose of the school that is built from individual purposes of the school. To be shared, the vision must be so clear that everyone understands it and will implement it in the same way. With this new vision, grade levels, programs, teachers, and staff members must make it come alive in their areas of purview. Communication and ongoing measurements are required to keep everyone working together toward this vision. Schools must make the time. The best method of getting to a shared vision through these steps is to make time for a retreat that will be facilitated by someone outside of the school, allowing everyone in the school to participate.

In brief, schools must make the time to—
* understand who their students are
* develop core values and beliefs, based on individual values and beliefs
* develop a clear purpose for the school that everyone agrees with and will commit to
* develop a shared vision built from the two points above and individual visions of the individuals in the school community
* document school processes and alter on the basis of data gathered
* gather and analyze data to understand the impact of instruction on student learning
* work together to implement new instructional and assessment strategies to improve student learning
* measure, measure, measure

Chapter 6
Quality Planning

Introduction to Quality Planning

Vision without action is merely a dream.
Action without vision just passes the time.
Vision with action can change the world.

Joel A. Barker

All organizations need a vision. All organizations must plan for the vision, or the vision will never be realized.

A well-defined and well-executed school improvement effort begins with a comprehensive schoolwide strategic plan that provides a logical framework for clarifying and achieving the vision. The school plan includes: an assessment of where the school is today and what factors can be expected to influence it in the future; a mission statement describing the school's purpose and function; a vision that reflects the values and beliefs of the individuals who make up the organization; long-range goals that make the intents of the mission and vision tangible; an identification of outcomes; a plan for evaluation and continuous improvement; an action plan that identifies the procedural steps needed to implement the goals, including timelines, responsibility, accountability; and, an estimation of budget needs based on the action plan.

SCHOOL **portfolio** PORTFOLIO

Quality Planning

This Quality Planning section is organized to add new information each year. The current sections are as follows:

Year One	Year Two	Year Three
• Student Expectations	• Refining the Guiding Principles of the School Values and Beliefs Purpose Mission Vision	• Vision
• Planning Time		• The Schoolwide Plan
• School Improvement Plan		• Planning Time
• The Title 1 Plan		• Looking Back on Year Three
• English Language Development Plan	• The Schoolwide Plan Study Team Results	• Next Steps
• Technology Plan	• Planning Time	
• District Plan to Upgrade Facilities	• Looking Back on Year Two	
• Budget	• Next Steps	
• Looking Back on Year One		
• Next Steps		

SCHOOL **portfolio** RTFOLIO

Quality Planning — Year One

Several years ago, River Road staff stated the following goals for our students: River Road students will—

- achieve academically
- be critical thinkers
- be able to work well independently, as well as interdependently
- perceive learning as a lifelong process
- have the skills, self-confidence, and values necessary to become contributing members of our society

Student Expectations

At the same time, staff identified the following nine student outcomes which represent skills our students need to acquire to be contributing members of society:

- Readiness to learn
- Literacy
- Critical thinking
- Problem-solving skills
- Collaborative skills
- Mastery of mathematics and scientific concepts
- Literacy in technology
- High personal and social efficacy
- An appreciation for lifelong learning

Planning Time

We do most of our planning after school. These after-school meetings include two faculty meetings per month, two grade-level meetings per month, plus ad hoc committee meetings and various district meetings. In  addition, we have six minimum days per year for planning and professional development. Since most of the time spent in meetings is beyond the normal workday, there is a constant conflict between using time to deal with problems versus using time for quality planning.

SCHOOL **portfolio** RTFOLIO

Schools too often will have several plans operating at one time, without a clear focus. In such a situation, students often experience school as incoherent.

School Improvement Plan

State and district requirements mandate an annual school plan. Each spring, a small committee is formed to create a school plan for the upcoming school year. Due to numerous commitments at the end of last year, committee members met on their own time in the summer. The plan was approved by staff at the first faculty meeting of the year and by the school site council at its September meeting.

The Title 1 Plan

The Title 1 committee revises its plan each year. These committee members include staff, administration, and several parents. In reality, we have not had as much direct parent involvement in this committee as we would like. Parent members have signed off on the plan each year after it is revised, but have not been directly involved in the revisions.

Because 89 percent of our student population is identified as Title 1 eligible, the Title 1 Plan controls a large part of our discretionary funding. It supports two Reading Recovery resource teachers, four paraprofessionals, and instructional materials earmarked for eligible students. This year, we used available funding to purchase computers to be placed in the Media Center. We also purchased learning modules that students will use to reinforce their learning.

English Language Development Plan

One of our teachers serves as the school liaison to the District English Language Development Committee, which developed the district plan to serve English language development needs of students. As part of that plan, the District provides six paraprofessionals to serve students at River Road. The District also pays for training in English language development for existing teachers. We recognize that we are out of compliance with state requirements that teachers of English language learners be certified.

With so many plans being juggled, it is easy to budget on a piecemeal basis. It is difficult to budget for the "big picture" of the school.

Technology Plan

Recognizing that technology can be a powerful tool in learning, we developed a technology plan last year. All teachers were given an opportunity to provide input to the technology committee before it began to write the plan. The technology committee was comprised of the principal, the library media specialist who is in charge of the computer lab, and an interested classroom teacher. This plan coordinates efforts with the district to bring technology into the classroom.

District Plan to Upgrade Facilities

The school bond that was passed three years ago has already resulted in upgraded electrical wiring to support technology. The district is expecting to have a districtwide network in operation by next year. A Local Area Network

(LAN) at the school site already connects the school office to the district. The new network will provide Internet access to computer labs and to classrooms next year. However, the school will be responsible for providing its own hardware and software. Our Technology Plan for year one is shown on the next page.

Budget

This year, the principal shared highlights of the budget with the staff, including how school improvement, Title I, and other funds would be allocated. The principal asked staff for input on special needs they may have that could be met with surplus funds.

SCHOOL portfolio RTFOLIO

This is an example of documentation that backs up the narrative in the school portfolio.

River Road Elementary School Technology Plan
Year One

Where we are right now

Hardware—

Year One: Purchase Macintosh computers and printers to complete ratio of one computer per classroom. All classrooms will have at least one CD-ROM drive. Add a scanner to library media center.

Year Two: Add a second computer in all fourth and fifth grade classrooms. If the district network is completed, connect all computers to the network.

Year Three: Add a second computer in all first, second, and third grade classrooms. Add a high capacity network printer in the media center.

Software—

Year One: Add student writing center software for all classrooms, if it is not currently available.

Year Two: For K-3 classrooms, add Kidpix, if it is not already available. For grades 4-5, add Hyperstudio, if not already available.

Year Three: Make sure all computers that are networked have appropriate Internet software (e.g., browser, e-mail.)

Staff Development—

• Encourage teachers to attend workshops and conferences on integrating technology.
• Provide on-site computer training after school.

YEAR ONE

SCHOOL portfolio PORTFOLIO

Once staff have the opportunity to reflect on their work using the Continuous Improvement Continuums, they often see the "holes" in their previous efforts at systemic change.

Schoolwide Planning is an excellent way to get set up with one plan to cover the "big picture" of the school.

Creating a diagram of current plans, reports, and funding initiatives can be very clarifying for staff trying to synthesize and prioritize efforts.

Looking Back on Year One

In assessing ourselves on the Education for the Future Initiative Continuous Improvement Continuums, we could see how scattered our work has been. Although our staff has done a considerable amount of work, everyone is moving in different directions and vying for scarce resources. We need to create a clearer vision of where we are going, and one overall plan to get there.

Next Steps

We need to—
- revisit our mission and create a clear vision
- research options for getting to the vision
- create a plan (same as Schoolwide Plan for IASA)
- establish a budget that is aligned to the plan
- create a process to monitor and implement the plan
- possibly work with community groups, using the same data we are collecting as the needs assessment for a Healthy Start grant (under consideration)

Since we have a large Title 1 population and a growing population of English language learners, we will take this opportunity to conduct schoolwide planning while we work on our school portfolio. The data we collect for our change efforts will be the same data we collect for our needs assessment under

the Improving America's Schools Act (IASA) guidelines. The school plan we create will be submitted as the Schoolwide Plan, allowing us to integrate funding sources to serve all students. We see this as a win-win for all our students.

SCHOOL **portfolio** RTFOLIO

Quality Planning — Year Two

Refining the Guiding Principles of the School

By the end of last year, we realized that our mission and nine student expectations were neither providing a clear direction for teachers nor increasing the achievement of students. We needed clarity on where we were going, and needed to make sure that we were all going in the same direction. We also knew that our mission and vision had to better meet the students we have in our school.

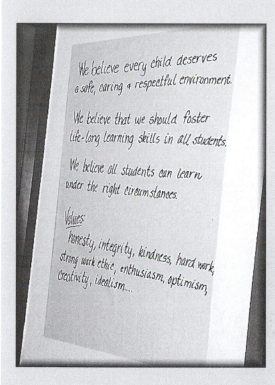

We believe every child deserves a safe, caring & respectful environment.

We believe that we should foster life-long learning skills in all students.

We believe all students can learn under the right circumstances.

Values:
honesty, integrity, kindness, hard work, strong work ethic, enthusiasm, optimism, creativity, idealism....

Over the summer, our partnership team took the lead in gathering the community together. Informal community conversations focused on what we want our children to know and be able to do and did much to raise the River Road school community's stake in developing a new vision and mission for the school.

We used a professional development day before school began in the fall, followed by a weekend retreat, to develop a shared vision that would reflect the data we collected, and the mission and purpose of the school built on our values and beliefs. Recognizing that we had to be productive in a limited time, we brought in a facilitator to help us.

We started the development of our values and beliefs, purpose, mission and vision by first clarifying our individual thoughts and merging these into collective thoughts. Our collective thoughts emerged as follows.

NOTES

Identifying values and beliefs is crucial in the development of a vision that will be truly shared. Values and beliefs are at the core of who we are, what we think and feel, and everything we do.

Values and Beliefs

We are very proud that we were able to craft values and beliefs for our school, based on our collective individual values and beliefs.

River Road Elementary School
Values and Beliefs

- We, as the school community, have a fundamental responsibility to make sure that all children develop literacy to their full potential.

- In order to foster students' innate curiousity, ability, and desire to learn and reach their potential, their basic needs must be met.

- All parents want their children to succeed; educating our children is the shared responsibility of parents, staff, and the broader community, all working together.

- Every child at River Road is an individual with unique needs, gifts, and learning styles. Each child has the desire and potential to learn. We are committed to providing an educational environment that supports all of the varied needs, gifts, and learning styles of our children.

- We must provide elementary school learners with concrete, hands-on experiences from which to build problem-solving skills.

- Technology can improve learning when it is well integrated into the curriculum and used to build upon real experiences.

- As a school and as individuals, we value the cultures and customs of our families.

SCHOOL *portfolio* RTFOLIO

NOTES

A mission statement needs to be brief, clear, focused, and describe the purpose and function of the school.

The work on the mission is not done when a statement has been agreed upon. The mission must be revisited annually, as individuals within the school change and as the school population changes.

A vision describes what the school will look like when the mission is accomplished.

Purpose

We determined that the purpose of River Road Elementary School is to do everything we can do to make sure students acquire the skills and knowledge that will allow them to be anything they want to be in the future.

Mission

The mission that evolved from the purpose and our values and beliefs follows.

> *The mission of River Road Elementary School is to provide all students with a positive, secure, and supportive learning environment in which they can acquire the skills and attitudes that foster an enjoyment of learning; respect for themselves and others; and, the physical, emotional, and social competencies necessary to become responsible and productive citizens of the 21st century.*

Vision

After we determined our values and beliefs and agreed on the purpose and mission of River Road Elementary School, each of us wrote our personal vision for the school. Prior to this retreat, we would have been terrified to have engaged in such an activity that could foster so many ideas and make us all vulnerable to never finishing the job. However, the clarity of our values and beliefs, who our students are and how they are performing, and the purpose of the school helped a shared vision emerge very quickly. We surprisingly had very similar ideas about the way we wanted to focus our efforts on our students and what we needed to be doing for them. Our vision was captured as shown on the next page.

Our next steps were to make meaning out of the vision at our grade levels and to ensure that our work builds on each other's work. In our grade-level meetings, we all wrote what the vision would look like, sound like, and feel like in our classrooms. We met together in our staff meetings and revised and revisited our interpretations of the vision. We are now clearer on what we need to be doing for the children.

YEAR TWO

SCHOOL **portfolio** PORTFOLIO

"Shared visions emerge from personal visions. This is how they derive their energy and how they foster commitment… If people don't have their own vision, all they can do is sign up for someone else's. The result is compliance, never commitment."

Peter Senge

A vision is a visual image of the mission. It needs to be written in practical, concrete terms that everyone can understand and see in the same way.

The River Road Elementary School Vision

River Road students will experience the curriculum through educational strategies to increase literacy and project-based learning that incorporates hands-on activities. The curriculum will also utilize cooperative learning strategies that encourage problem solving and enhance student abilities to work in teams.

Authentic assessment will be utilized to augment standardized tests. Authentic assessment will include student self-assessment and will be used as a tool for parent/teacher/student conferencing. Report cards will be tied to state and local standards. In addition to report cards, narratives and student portfolios will be used as part of the process for reporting student progress to parents, and for involving students in their own assessments.

Our commitment to change is exemplified by providing broad access to a myriad of technological resources. River Road teachers will integrate technology throughout the curriculum to help prepare students for the world of work. Computers and other advanced technologies will help develop students' critical thinking and problem-solving skills and will enable them to control their own learning and collaborate with other students.

Our families, staff, and community will work together to nurture and develop a deep appreciation for each other's cultures. The entire River Road school community will feel welcomed and appreciated at our school. Working in partnership with parents and community, we will ensure that individual student needs, gifts, and learning styles are respected and addressed. Students will leave River Road ready for future learning.

SCHOOL *portfolio* RTFOLIO

A comprehensive action plan defines the specific actions needed to implement the vision, sets forth when the actions will take place, and designates who is responsible for accomplishing the action.

The Schoolwide Plan

We recognize that we need a plan to make this vision a reality. We also know that if we do not know what the options are for implementing the vision, we will be doing the same things we have always done, putting us at risk of getting the same results we have always gotten. Therefore, study teams were established to investigate strategies we could implement that would help us achieve our vision. The study teams that were established include—

River Road Elementary School Study Teams
Year Two

- *Partnership*
  This study team is charged with creating opportunities for parents and community partners to get involved with the school in meaningful ways. Key components of this team's study will focus on parent education, coordination of social services, health agencies, and other community resources to support the River Road Elementary School vision.

- *Literacy*
  The literacy team is made up primarily of the people serving on the district literacy standards team. Their purpose is to develop a plan for attaining the standards by studying strategies that work for our students.

- *Standards-based Authentic Assessment*
  This study team is established to create plans to develop and implement authentic assessment tied to school and district standards.

- *Technology*
  Building on the technology plan developed last year, this study team's job is to refine the plan and tie it to our vision for learning.

- *Hands-on, Project-based Learning*
  This study team's focus is to investigate not only curriculum, such as Adopt-A-Watershed, but also the professional development needed to implement hands-on learning across the curriculum.

SCHOOL **portfolio** PORTFOLIO

Action planning is the process by which the school holds itself accountable for the actual implementation of the vision.

Lack of planning time is often an impediment to improvement. Therefore, the school must use creative solutions to the issue of time, as River Road did in year two.

Study Team Results

Each study team researched the best practices in their areas, and made recommendations for action. All recommendations were brought to the entire staff and school site council for approval. The school leadership team then took the approved recommendations and aligned them with the "next-steps" outlined in River Road's self-assessment on the Continuous Improvement Continuums. We recognize that their work to keep all plans focused and integrated is difficult but critical if we are to reach our vision. The leadership team prioritized the recommendations and took them back to the staff. A single, comprehensive plan is beginning to emerge from these efforts.

Planning Time

It became clear early in the year that we would not be able to do the necessary intensive work without creating planning time. We added ten minutes to instructional time, four days a week, and dismissed students 40 minutes early on Thursdays, providing us with two hours each week in which to plan together. This required a contract waiver from the teachers' contract, which was agreeable to both the teachers association and the district. For the first time, our staff meetings feel meaningful. They are about implementing a vision for the students, not about insignificant details that hold us hostage for months and even years. We have learned how to delegate work and expect the work to be accomplished and communicated back to everyone. We are learning how to collaborate and work together for the benefit of our students.

SCHOOL **portfolio** RTFOLIO

Looking Back on Year Two

This has been both a difficult and exciting year for us. We feel that we are finally rowing in the same direction and, if we stay on course in implementing this plan, we will see student achievement gains. We know that we have a long way to go, but at least the path is clear.

Next Steps

We will need to pay attention next year to keeping our energy high and staying focused. In terms of quality planning, our efforts now will go into—

- implementing the vision and plan
- monitoring and measuring our progress
- collecting data that will help us assess the impact of change
- improving our plan based upon data
- staying focused on the things that are important

SCHOOL *portfolio* PORTFOLIO

Quality Planning — Year Three

Vision

At the end of last year, everyone was very excited about the vision and plan we created. This year, the hard work that it takes to implement that vision became more clear, and we needed to continually celebrate small victories to keep the energy flowing (see Leadership). One of the important lessons of this year has been the realization that creating a quality plan is only the first step in implementing a vision. Through this work about ourselves, we learned about becoming real supporters of learning for students, and about being proactive rather than reactive. We learned how to create a way to get involved with parents, as opposed to creating a plan for getting parents involved. We learned why we could not implement our original ideals; these ideals had little to do with our students; they were about us. We learned that we were not going to show progress until we were clear on who our students are. We also learned that we have to do the hard work of understanding the results we are getting now, based on what we are implementing in our classrooms. We were grateful for having taken the time to build our team and recapture our school through the clarification of our values and beliefs and purpose before we dove into the planning. These principles always stayed at the core of our discussions and efforts, and kept us focused on them.

The Plan

During the planning process last year, study teams developed expertise in specific areas. Many of these teams felt that they had a stake in the implementation, and it was clear that the leadership team could not be responsible for implementing the plan alone. Implementation teams were formed to make sure staff had whatever was needed to implement the plan, including appropriate materials and professional development along with peer coaching. While most staff continued participating in implementation teams that were in their study team areas, everyone had the opportunity to change teams.

Implementation teams were formed in the following areas:
- Literacy
- Standards and Assessment
- Hands-on/project-based learning
- Technology
- Partnership Development

SCHOOL portfolio RTFOLIO

In the area of Partnership Development, in particular, there were several subteams formed that involved many parents and community members who were continuing their work from last year.

Each team took its area of the plan and created a workplan with the details needed for the year. The leadership team then reviewed the plans of each implementation team to make sure that the dates were realistic, especially with respect to items that impacted the entire staff. Once the details of the plans were finalized, we posted them in the faculty room and checked off items as they were completed.

Example of Planning Process

In the school plan under Student Achievement Goal 2, Standards and Assessment, we planned to use "student self-assessment through portfolios as part of parent conferences." To implement this goal, the standards and assessment action team defined their work for the year in the exhibit on the following page.

Planning Time

We have continued the revised student schedule which allows for collaborative planning time this year, and recognize that it will continue to be a necessity for moving the school forward. This time is now used primarily for working on the implementation of our school plan. Reculturing our school for change included defining norms of behavior and learning how to run effective meetings. Now our staff meeting times are devoted to our vision and not petty problems that one or two people could solve.

Looking Back on Year Three

We have developed an ongoing planning process that is intricately connected to both our vision and our leadership structure. We have made this process work for us.

Next Steps

- We need to continue to implement our schoolwide plan.
- We need to use data more to know how to improve our plans, especially in tracking students who have graduated to middle school.

Planning one year at a time never adds up to a complete vision. Start with the vision and work backward until there is a complete action plan to implement the vision.

Successfully implementing a vision is in part dependent upon a school's ability to operate effective meetings. Schools that continuously improve successfully run effective staff meetings that are focused on the implementation of the vision.

Data analysis will help the school understand the impact of changes made.

SCHOOL portfolio TFOLIO

It is important that the systems needed to implement the plan be developed by the time the plan is complete. For example, supportive leadership structures, partnerships, and professional development aimed at implementing the vision must be established for the plan to be successfully implemented throughout the organization.

In a real school's portfolio, the actual workplan documents would have been inserted here, and included a budget column.

River Road Elementary School Standards and Assessment Team Workplan		
What	**Who**	**When**
1. Pilot the use of a six-step rubric (developed last year) as a student self-assessment tool.	Cindy and action team—Joyce will coach as needed	Sept-Oct
2. Evaluate the pilot.	Cindy and action team (report to leadership team)	By October 20th
3. Make changes to rubric, if necessary, and pilot again.	Action team led by Joyce—all team members will pilot	November 20th
4. Train all teachers.	Team members through grade level meetings	December 15th
5. All teachers begin to use rubric with students. Keep writing samples and student self-assessments.	All teachers, with coaching offered by team members	By January 30th
6. Examine student work and self-assessments.	Whole staff led by Joyce	Third week in February
7. Begin to use student self-assessments as part of parent conferences.	All teachers	Spring parent conferences in April

Quality Planning Summary
from the Authors' Perspectives

River Road Progress

Starting with a different plan for everything they were doing, River Road soon realized that when they became clear on their vision, they only needed one plan to get to that vision. In fact, those multiple plans were more easily attainable when they could think about one plan related to one school vision.

The development of the vision was the key to effective quality planning at River Road Elementary School. After they itemized all they needed to do in order to implement the vision, they could see how they could integrate the different actions in order to decrease the amount of work they needed to complete the plan.

Items for the Quality Planning Section

Items that you might want to place in this Quality Planning section of your school portfolio:

- Assessments on the Education for the Future Initiative Quality Planning Continuous Improvement Continuum and discussion about priorities and next steps (River Road's appears in the Continuous Improvement and Evaluation section of their school portfolio)
- Descriptions of the school's—
  * Analysis of what needs to change, unless it can be found in another section
  * Purpose, mission, values, beliefs, vision
  * Description of how this vision will meet the needs of students
  * Goals
  * Improvement plan
  * Other plans or requirements of regulatory organizations
  * Strategic action plan
  * Budget plan
  * How the school plan was developed, how it was able to get the commitment of staff, and how it is used
  * Evidence of use of the overall school plan (implementation) and its effectiveness
  * Goals for next year in the area of planning
  * Analysis of what needs to happen to move up in the continuum

Making the Difference for Continuous Improvement

Understanding that a school has only one vision and therefore needs only one plan to get to the vision can be a relief for some schools that are trying to balance a myriad of plans. With one comprehensive school plan, priorities can be determined, elements can be leveraged, and a vision can be accomplished. All staff members can see how their work is part of the whole.

When schools plan to implement a clear, shared vision, they will see that things start happening at the school and changes begin to take place—faster than they ever thought possible. Planning for the vision is the only way to accomplish a vision. One-year plans, collectively, never add up to or equal the implementation of a vision. Schools will also quickly realize that they do not necessarily need additional dollars to implement a vision. First of all, if they are clear on a vision, all the other things they are doing that are not a part of that vision ends. Staff will find that they have about as much money as they have time to learn and implement new strategies.

Recommendations

In order to truly plan in a quality manner, schools must first be clear on a vision. Follow the steps in action planning, on the next page, to determine how a vision can be implemented and what it will take.

We also recommend that schools find time out of the school week to plan, communicate, and implement the vision, and to use most of the time they have together to work toward the implementation of the vision. Effective meetings are key.

Steps in Action Planning

1 List the school goals and any other required program goals (e.g., implement integrated instruction).

2 Below each goal, list the elements that need to be accomplished to implement the goal (i.e., derive student learning standards, provide teachers with professional development training in integrated instruction).

3 Identify any sub-elements that need to be accomplished within the context of each element (for example, professional development training might require "identify trainer" or "reserve meeting room"). Include any "next steps" from evaluations on the CICs that are not already in the plan.

4 Begin to arrange the elements and sub-elements required by each goal in chronological order. (Keep this version for later reference.)

5 Using the goals, elements, and sub-elements, begin fine-tuning the plan in chronological summary form, starting with the action to be taken first.

6 In a planning form, label columns—Action, Person Responsible, Due Date, and Timeline. Place the reorganized elements and sub-elements in the action column in a manner that is easiest for staff to utilize later. In the column next to each action, identify the person ultimately responsible for the action. Try not to use team names in the "person responsible" column. Accountability is most effective if the responsibility is delegated to an individual. Responsible persons determine how accountability reviews are conducted.

7 In the column next to Person Responsible, determine the Due Date. For each sub-element or element (depends on the topic and structure for implementation) determine when the activity absolutely must be completed.

8 In the columns that represent months, weeks, and sometimes days, make notations that will indicate when the activity will begin, its duration, and when it will be completed.

9 Determine how activities will be evaluated.

Chapter 7
Professional Development

Introduction to Professional Development

It's easy to get the players.
Getting 'em to play together,
that's the hard part.

Casey Stengel

Schools committed to improvement must reculture themselves for change. They must establish new systems for teamwork, communication, and collaboration. These schools must create new norms of behavior, and must develop leadership and continuous improvement skills in all employees. This process of creating a new school culture requires that teachers, principals, and staff be able to work well together—to communicate clearly and effectively with each other, and to trust and respect each other.

In effect, most schools working to improve are asking staff to change significantly the manner in which they work—how they make decisions; analyze and use data; plan for change; teach; monitor student achievement; evaluate and train personnel; and, assess the impact of new approaches to instruction and student assessment.

Improving schools also ask staff to change significantly the manner in which they think about work—to replace assumptions and hunches, especially about students and their learning, with facts; to open up their classroom doors and work with colleagues in teams; to consider their every action in terms of its impact on others and the school organization.

Ongoing professional development activities that are planned in congruence with the school goals and calendar provide school staff with opportunities both to improve personal performance and to learn the new skills they need to reform the school culture and support the development of a true learning organization.

SCHOOL **portfolio** RTFOLIO

Professional Development

This Professional Development section is organized to add new information each year. The current sections are as follows:

Year One	Year Two	Year Three
• Approach	• Approach	• Approach
• Content	• Content	• Content
• Impact	• Reculturing the School	• Impact
• Looking Back on Year One	• Impact	• Looking Back on Year Three
• Next Steps	• Looking Back on Year Two	• Next Steps
	• Next Steps	

SCHOOL **portfolio** RTFOLIO

NOTES

Before there is a clear plan, allotting days according to interest seems reasonable. Once a plan is in place, it becomes clear that the purpose of professional development is to build the capacity of all the individuals in the school to implement the vision and plan.

Professional Development — Year One

Approach

The administration at River Road has always been very generous in allowing staff to go to workshops and conferences based upon individual teacher's interests. This year, each teacher was allotted two days of release time to attend professional development workshops or conferences of their choice. We were asked to report what we learned during faculty meetings or at grade-level meetings.

In reviewing our attendance at conferences and workshops, we discovered that—

- over 50 percent of our teaching staff attended some sort of professional development workshop during this past year
- there are several staff members who do not attend workshops on a regular basis
- there are some staff members who claim they haven't attended any conferences or workshops for quite a few years. Many of these teachers do not like to leave their students with substitute teachers

The district provides six professional development days each year when students are not present. Two of these days are allocated to districtwide activities, while teachers can choose from a variety of workshops on the remaining four.

During this year, we struggled with making professional development more focused. Early literacy advocates on our staff shared the program at a faculty meeting to consider implementation schoolwide. It was voted down by two votes. The principal, however, suggested that those who wanted to implement the program could do so and that he would revise the budget to support the program. Although some teachers were happy with the decision, others felt there should be a different process for implementing professional development programs.

This became a bigger issue three months later when two teachers addressed the faculty about more widespread training in the Adopt-a-Watershed program.

SCHOOL portfolio RTFOLIO

NOTES

In the absence of a clear schoolwide focus, the work of the more committed staff tends to go in many competing directions, while giving others an excuse not to participate.

These teachers felt that Adopt-a-Watershed would be a good complement to hands-on science, provide motivating source material for students' writing, and introduce service learning. The principal wanted to be supportive, but he had been told the day before that the district plans to train K-5 teachers in hands-on math next year. Teachers were not willing to give up the smorgasbord of choices they have traditionally had in order to target our work as a school.

These events caused us to have heated debates about priorities in professional development, district focus versus site focus, and the need for a better way to decide a focus. It was decided in May of year one that a team would be formed to study the issue when school starts in September.

Content

This year, the two district professional development days that were common to all, involved one day of hands-on science from Everystate University, and a day of diversity training. Other professional development activities attended by our teachers included—
- new approaches to teaching and motivating students
- language arts standards
- Reading Recovery
- journal writing
- authentic assessment
- systems thinking
- hands-on science
- Pee-Wee Math
- technology
- early literacy development
- new spelling programs
- Southeast Asian customs and culture
- Adopt-A-Watershed

Impact

Several teachers have reported great success with students when using the strategies and programs they learned in professional development this past year. One grade one teacher used early literacy intervention and two grade three teachers developed and used authentic assessments in languages arts and math. A few teachers onsite have become proficient with the use of technology in their classrooms. Two teachers have implemented the Adopt-A-Watershed

SCHOOL portfolio RTFOLIO

Working together, the staff can do so much more than the sum of all the individuals working separately.

curriculum, and many are implementing hands-on science. Teachers feel that they get good ideas from the professional development they attend, but sessions are far too varied to implement everything.

Looking Back on Year One

There are many talented teachers in this school. If we were all implementing strategies and programs in common, we could provide substantial support for each other and impact student achievement much more. Before we can focus our professional development, we need to become clearer about the focus of the school and where we are headed.

Next Steps

Once we are clear on our vision and have a plan to get to there, we will align professional development with the plan.

SCHOOL **portfolio** RTFOLIO

Professional Development — Year Two

Approach

At the beginning of year two, we were focused on establishing a schoolwide vision, and revising our leadership and decision-making processes. It was decided that the professional development issues that surfaced in year one be addressed and resolved using shared decision-making. We realized that the selection of professional development activities needed to be consistent across staff and connected to the shared purpose of the school.

Once the school vision, mission, and one school plan were established, our study teams researched strategies and programs to determine what would best meet our students' needs. Instead of using all our professional development time to participate in workshops, we used most of it to work in teams to build our own capacity for change. We started to look at how to collect data and what data to collect over time to know if these new strategies were making a difference with student achievement.

We needed to create time to do this important work, which we found in a variety of ways:

- The district agreed to allow us to use four of the six staff development days each year at the school level.
- Our principal restructured faculty meetings so that one of the two each month could be used for professional development.
- Once the school plan was finished, much of the weekly planning time was used to implement the plan, some of which was used for professional development.
- Release time was used when a small group of teachers was involved.
- Teachers continued to go to conferences, but chose conferences based on the relevance to implementing our school plan.

Each time we assess where we are on the Continuous Improvement Continuums we study the effect of professional development on student achievement.

NOTES

Using data to understand the impact of instructional processes on student learning helps teachers understand what to change to get different results.

When schools have a plan and a vision, it is much easier to get the buy-in of the district to allow schools to do things differently.

SCHOOL portfolio RTFOLIO

A "real" school would include actual documentation of this work as evidence in their school portfolio.

Schools committed to improvement must reculture themselves for change, so new ways of working can be implemented. Determining norms of behavior, how to run effective meetings, and how to reach consensus are major elements of reculturing schools.

Content

We focused our professional development in the four student learning goal areas: early literacy; standards and assessment; technology; and, hands-on learning. However, rather than treat these as separate, we posed several questions that encouraged staff to see the connections.

For example—
How can we connect hands-on learning to the literacy standards using technology as a tool in the process?

We developed training around these questions using the expertise of our own staff. Training included group work to translate the implementation of the work to all grade levels and across grade levels.

Some of the highlights of professional development this year include—

- using study teams to develop a long-term plan based on our vision
- implementing early literacy using Reading Recovery strategies
- incorporating hands-on learning through Adopt-A-Watershed curriculum and hands-on math (district)
- providing technology training in multimedia as a method for students to record their work
- providing technology coaching in the classroom from our technology coordinator

Reculturing the School

In addition to working on student learning, we needed to use professional development time to change *how* we work and how we communicate with each other. We put considerable effort this year into developing shared decision-making, creating norms of behavior, running effective meetings, and creating a culture to support peer coaching. We also read and learned more about our students and their cultures.

SCHOOL **portfolio** RTFOLIO

"You cannot continuously improve interdependent systems and processes until you progressively perfect interdependent, interpersonal relationships."
Stephen Covey

Our norms of behavior are—
- Each member of this school will strive to understand the other person before trying to be understood.
- We will not make assumptions. We will ask for clarification.
- We will not talk behind each other's backs.
- There will be no cross-talk in open meetings.
- Feelings will be expressed openly, without judgement.
- There is no such thing as failure; there are only results.
- There are win-win solutions to every problem. We will find them.
- Our commitment is to help every student succeed. All of our actions are focused on this commitment.
- We value trust and will act with trustworthiness.

One benefit of this effort was the comfort level teachers experienced having a technology coordinator in the classrooms to model the use of technology. It happened that we had started coaching in an area where teachers were not expected to have expertise and they were, therefore, more willing to accept help. Now that teachers have had a positive experience with coaching, they are more willing to accept the practice in other areas.

Impact

For the first time, we are seeing instructional strategies implemented broadly across classrooms this year, related to professional development. We believe that the change is related to the vision, to the focused nature of professional development, and to the new expectation that all teachers will implement what they have learned in professional development.

SCHOOL *portfolio* PORTFOLIO

Peer coaching combined with the acquisition of new teaching skills is an expedient, positive, and supportive way for teachers to implement new strategies in the classroom.

Looking Back on Year Two

By the end of year two, our professional development efforts have become more targeted to making specific, schoolwide changes. We now want to move to more collaborative work in developing and implementing instructional units, and using peer coaching to improve our classroom strategies. We also would like to document in our school portfolio the impact of our professional development efforts on student achievement results and school processes.

Next Steps

- Make sure that all teachers know how to use the student database to identify weaknesses in the program and to input diagnostic assessments.
- Train all K-3 teachers in the use of Reading Recovery strategies.
- Continue peer coaching in technology, and begin to use it to implement Reading Recovery strategies in all K-3 classrooms.

SCHOOL portfolio RTFOLIO

Professional Development — Year Three

Approach

At the beginning of the year, the professional development action team analyzed student achievement and school process data and made recommendations to the staff and leadership team regarding modifications in the professional development components of our school plan. The modifications were primarily in the mode of delivery, rather than the content of professional development.

In the past two years, our approach to professional development has changed significantly. We are relying less and less on expensive conferences and workshops in which only one or two staff members benefit. Instead we have invested in activities in which the whole staff may share. Our staff looks in-house first when it needs expertise. This method not only increases staff self-esteem and is cost effective, it seems to be more effective in changing instructional practices.

This year, we continued to use internal experts but spent less time using a workshop format and more time collaborating in small groups and utilizing peer coaching. While this change had been our goal, it was propelled forward when staff development days were cut back. As a result, we had to rely more heavily on release time and on the weekly collaborative planning time we created last year by banking time.

Content

Through our decision-making structure, we reaffirmed the allocation of resources in several key areas:

- providing peer coaching in Reading Recovery strategies, including teaching decoding skills in the upper grades where needed
- continuing technology coaching in the classroom, in after-school workshops, and help as needed during planning time
- sharing hands-on math and science units, working together to infuse technology into the units, and working collaboratively to implement the units
- learning to use our database for action research
- understanding the culture of our students and community

NOTES

Changing the way professional development is conducted at a school, from a cafeteria approach to a collaborative approach to implementing the vision, is an indication of true change at the deepest level of the organization.

SCHOOL **portfolio** PORTFOLIO

Impact

We are seeing growth in reading among students who have been in our program for two or more years. We attribute this at least in part to the ability of classroom teachers to use Reading Recovery strategies, since the impact is not confined to students working directly with the Reading Recovery teachers.  Technology is being used to support the curriculum, and there is much more hands-on teaching and learning occurring in our classrooms. We believe that this positively impacts student learning based on student journals, questionnaire results, and discussions. We know that parents are pleased with the results of our work, and teachers believe that they are seeing results in terms of how students attack problems and how they perform on standardized assessments.

Looking Back on Year Three

We have worked very hard in the area of professional development in an effort to provide all staff with opportunities to work in teams, to continuously set and implement goals, and to use peer coaching to improve teaching skills. While effective teaching strategies related to the vision are not 100 percent evident in all classrooms, the majority of teachers feel supported in their efforts. All teachers do know, however, that professional development is about learning what we need to know to implement the vision of the school.

Next Steps

- Increase peer coaching to involve all teachers.
- Improve collaboration across grade levels.
- Use action research to improve teaching and learning.
- Support upper-grade staff to improve the teaching of reading.
- Implement professional development specifically to train new teachers to help them be able to understand who our students are, how to understand the impact of instructional processes on the students, and how to change processes to help all students learn.

Professional Development Summary from the Authors' Perspectives

River Road Progress

River Road staff significantly changed their way of thinking about professional development over these three years. As they began this work on their school portfolio, each member of the school could choose to go to whatever conference or workshop they wanted to, or they could chose to not go at all. By the end of two years, when the vision was clear and shared, they chose to work in groups to give meaning to their roles and responsibilities with respect to the vision, and to ensure the implementation of the vision in all aspects of the school. Everyone in the organization was committed and ready to implement that vision by year three. Any teachers new to the school were brought in "through" this vision.

The next steps River Road took with respect to professional development will greatly impact the student achievement results they are currently getting and should lead to impressive improvements. Those steps, peer coaching and teacher action research, will ensure that the vision will be implemented in all parts of the school.

Another very positive action that River Road took was that when they were clear on their vision, instead of doing the same things they have always done, they set up study teams to learn about new strategies and how to get better results. They studied how other schools have been working with similar populations and getting excellent results. They then reconstituted the study teams into implementation teams to ensure the implementation of these aspects in every classroom.

Items for the Professional Development Section

Items that might go in this Professional Development section of your school portfolio include:

- Assessments on the Education for the Future Initiative Professional Development Continuous Improvement Continuum and discussion about priorities and next steps (River Road's appears in the Continuous Improvement and Evaluation section of their school portfolio)
- Examples of student work (most probably placed in the Student Achievement section) that show implementation of new teaching strategies
- Description of the current approach to professional development, including implementation components

- Plan for professional development, including teacher outcomes
- How the plan was determined and how it will assist with school change
- Types of professional development needed to implement the school improvement plan, tied to the mission and vision, and taking into account teacher's individual goals
- Incentives for teachers to want to change current practices
- Professional development calendar for the year, with evidence that time is allotted for professional development
- Structure for communication in the school
- Norms of behavior
- Evaluation of effectiveness of professional development training and implementation
- Evidence that new skills are being implemented
- Budget reflecting professional development needs (described in Quality Planning)
- Teacher and staff performance evaluation processes
- Plans for improvement
- Photos of staff supporting each other in implementing new ways of teaching and communicating

Making the Difference for Continuous Improvement

Again, having the vision, commitment of staff, and the leadership to implement this vision makes all the difference in the world in *entire* staffs implementing a continuum of learning that makes sense for students. Appropriate and strong professional development focused on the implementation of the vision will help schools make changes to implement the vision.

Firstly, professional development can help reculture the school for change, build collaborative teams, norms of behavior, and collegial partners. Secondly, professional development can help everyone understand their role in implementing the vision and how their role works with everyone else's role. Thirdly, professional development can support the implementation of the vision with accountability and time.

Recommendations

As schools begin the school improvement process, we highly recommend that staff commit to some sort of retreat to reculture their school for change, to build teams of collaborative and collegial partners, and to develop that shared vision. We also recommend that new instructional approaches to implement be studied, and that collegial coaching be used with the new content knowledge to implement that vision. Again, data will make the difference in getting staff to continue to implement the vision when they see progress and the results.

Recommendations for effective professional development training that lead to successful school improvement and real change in the classroom are:

- Make sure the content, approach, and efficacy of the training will help the school reach its vision.
- Make sure everyone shares the same vision, and knows what she or he is expected to implement.
- Plan and schedule the training well in advance.
- Add a support and implementation component that has an element of accountability, and provides the time to use it effectively.
- Determine incentives for committing staff to ongoing, long-term professional development.
- Make sure all staff are involved in appropriate professional development.

Chapter 8
Leadership

Introduction to Leadership

*An essential factor in leadership is
the capacity to influence and organize
meaning for the members of the organization.*

Tom Peters

In order for schools to become true learning organizations, they must put into place a formal leadership infrastructure that allows necessary improvements—from within the organization and supported outside of the organization. A quality leadership infrastructure emphasizes the prevention of problems (such as student failure) as opposed to short-term fixes or the covering up of problems, and focuses on the creation of a learning organization that encourages everyone to contribute to making school have a cumulative, purposeful effect on student learning.

Before a meaningful and useful leadership infrastructure can be put into place, there must be an agreed upon purpose for the school; an understanding of the values and beliefs about teaching and learning held by the individuals who make up the school; a mission; and, there must be a clearly defined vision shared by these individuals.

Systemic school improvement requires understanding and implementing many new and interrelated components at the same time. Shared decision-making and site-based management are structural approaches to school leadership that, when used in conjunction with each other, allow individuals within the organization to create and maintain an effective learning organization.

The evolving roles of the school leaders and teams are extremely important in developing and maintaining a leadership infrastructure that will ensure the comprehensive implementation of the school vision. The school leadership structure must look like the school vision.

Note. From *The School Portfolio: A Comprehensive Framework for School Improvement*, Second Edition (p.125), by Victoria L. Bernhardt, 1998, Larchmont, NY: Eye on Education. Copyright © 1998 Eye on Education, Inc. Reprinted with permission.

SCHOOL **portfolio** PORTFOLIO

Leadership

This Leadership section is organized to add new information each year. The current sections are as follows:

Year One	Year Two	Year Three
• Shared Decision-making	• Shared Decision-making	• Shared Decision-making
• Decision-making Structure	• Shared Decision-making Structure	• The Leadership Structure
• Committee Structure	• The Leadership Team	• The Leadership Team
• Decision-making Process	• Committee Structure	• The District
• Looking Back on Year One	• Decision-making Process	• Looking Back on Year Three
• Next Steps	• Preparing for Implementation in Year Three	• Next Steps
	• Looking Back on Year Two	
	• Next Steps	

SCHOOL **portfolio** PORTFOLIO

"If a school is to foster educated citizenry for a democracy, then the school itself must be an example of a democracy... The substance of a school democracy are the decisions that improve the education of students, both collectively and individually, and the quality of educational life for the entire school community."

Carl Glickman

Leadership—Year One

Shared Decision-making

Our River Road principal, Mr. Young has been our lead decision-maker and principal for seven years. For years, staff were comfortable with school decisions being made by the principal and district administration. However, with increased demands for higher student achievement and accountability at the classroom level, more teachers are expecting to be involved in the decision-making process.

Some teachers believe that all decisions should be made by the faculty, some feel that it is the administration's responsibility, while others feel that some decisions belong to staff and other decisions belong to the administration.

Our principal believed that because he made all decisions in the past, he should maintain control of the process, seeking input from the staff as he deemed appropriate. He was skeptical of opening up the process, knowing that he would ultimately be held responsible for decisions. There was quite a bit of discussion about this during the first two months of the school year without any resulting change.

As the year continued, the principal became more open to shared decision-making and agreed to involve the staff in the following areas:
- classroom supplies and instructional materials
- scheduling assemblies and special events
- scheduling Title I instructional assistants' time

After our self-assessment on the Education for the Future Continuous Improvement Continuums, everyone, including Mr. Young, recognized that we needed greater staff buy-in if decisions were to lead to substantial school

SCHOOL **portfolio** PORTFOLIO

NOTES

Once agreed upon, a picture of your leadership structure will help everyone conceptualize how decisions are made in your school.

improvement. First, we broadened the scope of shared decision-making by consensus. Additions to those items mentioned earlier now include:

- facilities usage (library, multipurpose room, etc.)
- student discipline
- curriculum, to the degree that it is determined at the school
- instructional strategies

Decision-making Structure

A decision-making structure was designed to clarify how decisions would be made and by whom. Essentially, we now use ad hoc committees to come up with recommendations to the whole staff. This leadership structure is shown in Figure 30.

Figure 30
Leadership Structure—Year One

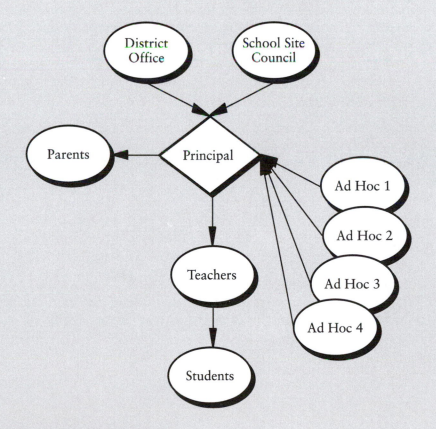

SCHOOL portfolio PORTFOLIO

NOTES

*Committees help get things
done. Schools are excellent
at establishing committees.
Schools are not as good
about disbanding them
when the jobs get done.*

*Anytime a committee is
formed, all members must
agree and abide by "Norms
of Behavior," as well as
meeting etiquette,
brainstorming rules, etc.
This will set a positive tone
for collaboration and will
keep the committee focused
on its goals. (See page 109,
Norms of Behavior example,
in "The School Portfolio: A
Comprehensive Framework
for School Improvement,"
Second Edition. For other
guidelines, see "Data
Analysis for Comprehensive
Schoolwide Improvement,"
pages 145-147.)*

Committee Structure

As issues arose, we formed committees of volunteers to study the topics and to make recommendations to staff. Every time a problem came up, we added a committee and never dropped or re-established existing committees. By late spring, staff began to realize that this process was having some negative side effects. The process resulted in the same teachers volunteering to be on committees, doing the research, and making the recommendations, leaving some teachers uninvolved. At times, this silent minority was even undermining and sabotaging decisions that were already made. Additionally, there were too many subcommittees formed with too little overall direction from staff. As a result, recommendations were often in conflict with each other.

Decision-making Process

We agreed to use a consensus model for shared decision-making, but found it terribly cumbersome. We realized almost right away that we needed some training to make this work! Occasionally, we would work at achieving consensus only to find that one person would block the decision. Then, we would end up sending the recommendation back to the committee, or deciding to just vote instead. We still believe in the concept of shared decision-making, but implementation is not as simple as we thought.

Looking Back on Year One

By the end of the school year, we realized that our decision-making structure was mostly reactive to real or perceived problems or to state, district, and federal mandates. We also realized that decision-making is not really shared unless we—

- have broad involvement of all the staff
- have a consensus process that we all understand
- all share some guiding principles that we can revisit when we disagree

We want to become proactive in making our work help us continuously improve the education experiences for students. We realize that our shared decision-making structure must evolve from a shared vision. Only then will we be able to use the process to focus on continuous improvement and getting everyone involved.

SCHOOL portfolio RTFOLIO

No leadership structure can be effective if staff is not committed to working together for the benefit of the students.

Next Steps

- We need to read the research on shared decision-making and understand the process better.
- We first need to spell out our beliefs and values, vision, mission, and shared goals, and then create a leadership structure that is congruent with these guiding principles.
- In creating a leadership structure, we need to incorporate communication processes that will keep everyone involved and informed.
- We need to come to consensus that the purpose of sharing decision-making is to advocate for the interests of all students. Without this agreement, we will continue to argue issues based on individual interests.

SCHOOL portfolio PORTFOLIO

NOTES

A quality professional development workshop on shared decision-making can help a school establish a workable leadership structure and reculture the school for change.

The process of clarifying shared guiding principles of the school can help build a culture that is focused on students.

Leadership — Year Two

Shared Decision-making

The results of our year one self-assessment on the Continuous Improvement Continuums, and the results of the parent, student, and teacher questionnaires helped us know we needed to create a shared mission and vision, based on shared purposes, values, and beliefs.

Before school began in the fall, we spent a professional development day followed by a weekend retreat to create these guiding principles. Our challenge  during the year was to create one school plan for implementing the vision. To do this, we needed a leadership committee structure that involved everyone and allowed us to achieve a great deal of work together. We were surprised how easily that structure flowed from our common mission, vision, and long-term goals. Our guiding principles helped us become more proactive and more focused, and we were able to avoid much of the contention that existed in decision-making last year.

In response to these changes, the principal openly shared how he had developed the budget. Teachers were surprised and pleased that the principal initiated this openness, and, for the most part, were satisfied that the budget was fair and equitable. Everyone understood that once a plan was in place, the budget would be re-examined and aligned to the plan.

Decision-making Structure

This year's leadership structure, which we used in developing the school plan, is shown in Figure 31.

SCHOOL *portfolio* RTFOLIO

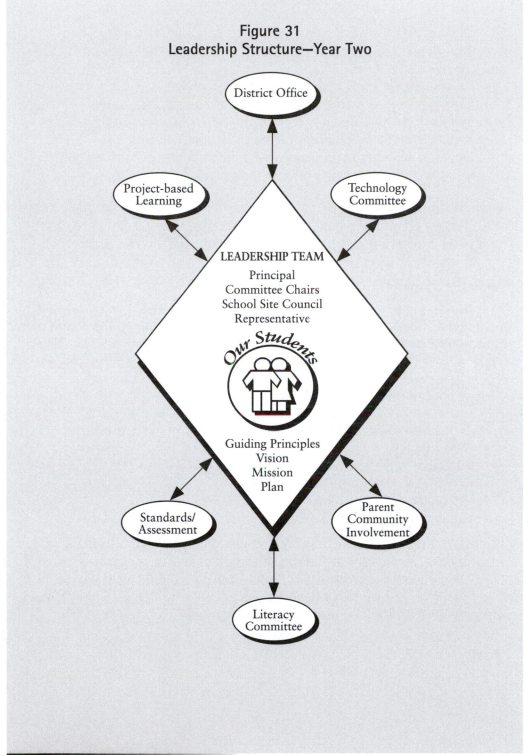

**Figure 31
Leadership Structure—Year Two**

District Office

Project-based
Learning

Technology
Committee

LEADERSHIP TEAM

Principal
Committee Chairs
School Site Council
Representative

Our Students

Guiding Principles
Vision
Mission
Plan

Standards/
Assessment

Parent
Community
Involvement

Literacy
Committee

NOTES

If the purpose of leadership is to implement the vision, the school's long-term goals and vision should be evident in its leadership structure.

YEAR TWO

SCHOOL **portfolio** RTFOLIO

NOTES

A committee structure that addresses the core work of the school ensures broad participation and staff buy-in.

Study teams are often established to study new approaches to doing business, and implementation teams are formed to implement the vision. Some schools attempt to use their study team structures to implement the vision. This is problematic. Mixing the constituency of teams will help make sure all aspects of the vision are implemented by everyone.

The Leadership Team

A leadership team, made up of the principal and leaders of each of the action teams, was established to—

- coordinate the work of the different committees
- keep everyone informed about the work of all the committees
- integrate the findings and recommendations of the committees
- schedule time during faculty meetings for discussion of recommendations as they were being developed to allow for input into the recommendation early in the process

It was the responsibility of the leadership team members to inform their teams of leadership team discussions, and to bring concerns back to the leadership team to be dealt with before these concerns became full blown disputes.

Committee Structure

We created teams to study approaches to implementing the vision and to recommend a plan within each area because we really wanted the action plan to be owned by everyone in the same way that the vision was shared. We also felt that if we could effectively communicate each team's learnings, the entire school community could grow as a result. The study teams in essence became the backbone of the decision-making structure.

Study teams were created for the five focus areas in our vision:
- early literacy
- standards and assessment
- parent and community involvement
- technology
- hands-on, project-based learning

The role of the study teams, each with representation of all grade levels, was to investigate different approaches to achieving our goal in the given focus area. They recommended specific instructional strategies and the staff development that would be needed to implement a high quality instructional program aligned with the district's emerging curriculum standards.

SCHO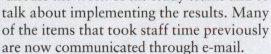OL PORTFOLIO

NOTES

Principals and team leaders must understand that "An essential factor in leadership is the capacity to influence and organize meaning for the members of the organization."

Tom Peters

Decision-making Process

After last year's difficulty in getting started with shared decision-making, we scheduled a day after the vision was developed for a shared decision-making workshop. Although the facilitator helped us create our leadership structure, the emphasis was on consensus building. As staff became more proficient in running effective meetings and coming to consensus, we all became convinced that we were on the right path.

Staff meetings and early release time were also used to communicate the results of the research taking place and to generate ideas about integrating the approaches.

Study teams met on the fourth Tuesday of every month. Their meetings were scheduled to complement staff meetings on the first and third Tuesdays of the month, and leadership team meetings on the second Tuesday of the month. Staff meeting times are now used to discuss the work of the study teams and to

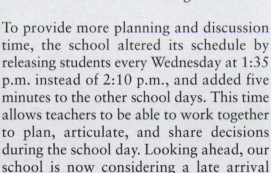

talk about implementing the results. Many of the items that took staff time previously are now communicated through e-mail.

To provide more planning and discussion time, the school altered its schedule by releasing students every Wednesday at 1:35 p.m. instead of 2:10 p.m., and added five minutes to the other school days. This time allows teachers to be able to work together to plan, articulate, and share decisions during the school day. Looking ahead, our school is now considering a late arrival time for students once a week, as opposed to early release, in order for staff to work on student achievement and curriculum planning in the morning hours.

Preparing for Implementation in Year Three

Late in the spring, after the school plan was completed, we changed the leadership structure to focus on implementation, as shown in Figure 32 on the following page.

SCHOOL **portfolio** PORTFOLIO

The leadership structure should facilitate the involvement and professional growth of all of the staff through participation in the learning community.

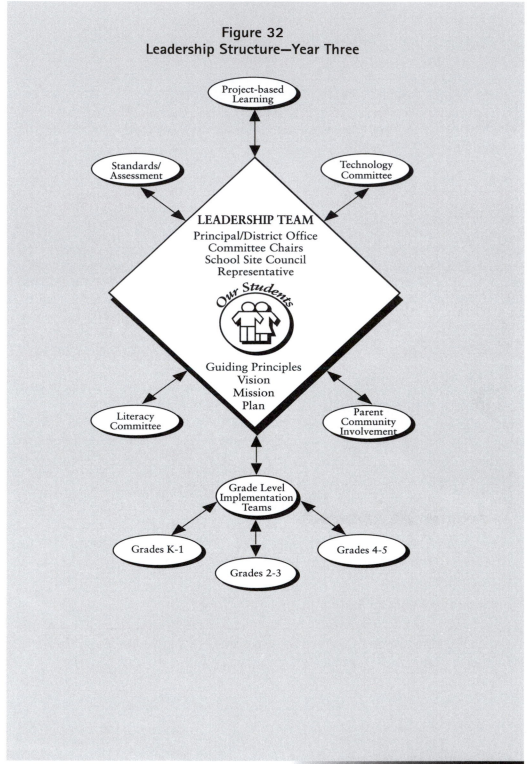

Figure 32
Leadership Structure—Year Three

LEADERSHIP

SCHOOL **portfolio** RTFOLIO

The inclusion of grade-level implementation teams reflects the understanding that implementation at the classroom level will ultimately depend upon peer collaboration and support. This is most likely to occur when teachers who work at the same level work together toward implementation. The role of the study teams will continue to be in the area of developing and refining strategies and curriculum, while the grade-level teams will concentrate on implementation. We will find out next year how well our concept works in practice.

Looking Back on Year Two

River Road staff made great strides in year two, by establishing a vision, an effective leadership structure, and by successfully making major decisions using the new shared decision-making process. A new implementation structure has been established, but the roles and responsibilities of each individual needs to be clarified.

Next Steps

- We need to use the implementation structure to implement our plan to get to the vision.
- We need to identify roles and responsibilities of every member of the organization, so that we can continue to learn and grow together.
- We need to stay focused!

SCHOOL portfolio RTFOLIO

Leadership — Year Three

Shared Decision-making

In year three, shared decision-making has become River Road's strong suit. Our shared decision-making structure is operating in a way that makes sense to everyone.

All decisions are based on our guiding principles. Whenever we come to a point of deciding whether to go one way or the other, we revisit our guiding principles, and we know exactly which way the decision must be made. The rule of thumb with our decision-making structure is: when a potential decision will impact others, those people need to be involved in the decision. For instance, if a decision is pending that would impact all staff members, that decision would need to be considered by the leadership team and then presented to the full staff. There are times when the principal makes decisions on his own, and times when teachers in their action teams need to make decisions that impact only their grade levels or content areas. Even if the leadership team is not utilized to make a decision, all action team decisions are reported to the leadership team and most of the time to the full staff. Our principal continues to handle the day-to-day responsibility for the school's operations, while the district maintains a certain degree of control over personnel hiring and accounting systems. We have worked with the district and other schools in creating standards and assessments.

The Leadership Structure

We continued to use the leadership structure that we developed at the end of last year for implementation. Early in the year, we found that the structure worked very well for getting work accomplished and involving the staff, but not as well as we had hoped for keeping everyone informed and making sure that the changes were being implemented at the classroom level. Since the leadership team is supposed to make sure that these things occur, we needed to take a closer look at its functioning.

SCHOOL PORTFOLIO

The Leadership Team

The leadership team is made up of the leaders of each action team. Action teams include classroom and resource teachers, classified staff, and, when possible, parents and students. Until mid-year, the principal was the head of the leadership team. Although he is crucial to our change efforts, he was the first to see that the demands of his role as manager of the school were conflicting with the time he needed to do an effective job as the primary change agent. Therefore, during the year, we named Cynthia Varicelli as our reform coordinator, the leader of our leadership team, and maintainer of our school portfolio. Released half-time from classroom duties, the coordinator prioritizes ideas, issues, and tasks, and makes sure the appropriate action teams receive the issues and move forward on them. The coordinator sets agendas for staff and leadership meetings and organizes the flow of the work. The coordinator also ensures the implementation of the vision in every classroom by arranging for peer collaboration and coaching. We are hoping to get a professional development grant next year that would allow us to release Cynthia full-time to coordinate peer coaching and to take over classes when teachers are coaching each other.

The District

District administrators and especially the superintendent have been supportive of our process and progress, but have not had direct participation, unless invited for a meeting or event. We would like a district administrator to become our school coach so the district can understand our vision and help implement it. Many of the waivers from district obligations that we have applied for have been granted—especially now that we have the school portfolio. It is clear to the administrators what we are trying to do. They report that it is clear that we have a plan and are following it.

NOTES

When feasible, it is a good idea to assign someone other than the principal to coordinate the schoolwide improvement effort. A principal's time can get eaten up by other things. Sometimes, however, the principal is the best person for that job.

Schools are wise to bring the district along with their shared decision-making evolution. Schools need district support and understanding.

SCHOOL **portfolio** PORTFOLIO

Looking Back on Year Three

After three years, there is no doubt in the principal's mind that shared decision-making is the best form of governance for a school seeking to continuously improve higher achievement for all students. Teachers appreciate staff meetings because they are focused on implementing the school vision. They are well organized, run smoothly, and are a very effective and efficient use of everyone's time. Much of the work is now done in committee, and the committees have learned when they need to seek input from staff so that everyone is on board when the final decision is made. Since we all know how to use a consensus process, decision-making is much less difficult than it used to be, and we are able to do more in less time. We still need to bring the community in more on our decision-making process so that the work of the staff and the work of our parent community become completely aligned.

Next Steps

- We need more involvement from the school community in planning and implementing school goals.
- We need to ask a district administrator to become our school coach so the district can understand and support all that we are doing and help guide us.
- We need to continue to support and create a collaborative school community atmosphere.
- We need an ongoing evaluation process to ensure that our leadership structure continues to support the vision and mission of the school.

Leadership Summary
from the Authors' Perspectives

River Road Progress

River Road made tremendous progress in the area of Leadership during these three years. Once they were clear that they wanted shared decision-making and, that in order for the structure to support them, they needed to have a shared vision, they were on the road to success. The River Road shared decision-making structure became a picture of their vision. Staff clarified who would do what and when to implement the vision. They learned how to delegate, how to assign responsibilities, and expected to see things get done. It became the way they do business. Perhaps the one thing that helped staff the most, besides getting the shared vision, was their adjustments in their weekly and daily schedules to provide time for planning and talking about the vision. Staff banked time to allow for student-free time to plan and communicate. Committee and staff meetings became efficient and focused on implementing the vision.

Items for the Leadership Section

The Leadership section of your school portfolio is where staff describe their leadership structure and how it works. Items that might go in this section include—

- Assessments on the Education for the Future Initiative Leadership Continuous Improvement Continuum (River Road's appears in the Continuous Improvement and Evaluation section of their school portfolio)
- Analysis of what needs to happen to move to the next levels in the continuum
- Shared decision-making structure and process—picture and description
- Types of decisions made at the school and analysis of who makes what decisions
- Roles and responsibilities of action teams, staff, principal, leader/coordinator, superintendent, and district office
- How staff meeting time is used—might include meeting structure, calendar, minutes
- Approach to consensus building
- Outcomes/benefits/strengths of approach
- Goals for improvement

Making the Difference for Leadership Continuous Improvement

The job of leaders is to help everyone in the organization understand her/his role in implementing the vision. The principal is not the only leader, and therefore, agreements about who makes what decisions, when, is crucial. When the vision is clear and shared, a leadership structure that looks like the vision will assist everyone in implementing the vision. A leadership structure that is not congruent with the vision will keep staff from implementing the vision.

When leadership structures are clear, staff will need to make time to implement the leadership structure. When school staffs are clear on roles and responsibilities and everyone is dedicated to shared decision-making, staff meetings become focused on implementing the vision. All other decisions are determined through various means, such as delegation, e-mail, and committee work.

Recommendations

If you want to know if everyone in your school understands, in the same way, how decisions are made at the school, have them independently draw a picture of the current leadership structure as each staff member experiences it. This will tell you if your leadership structure is clear and shared. If it is not, work together to build a common structure based on your school vision.

What is necessary to get a clear, shared leadership structure? Clearly a vision is required before an effective shared decision-making structure can be established. Most schools require supportive training to learn how to make decisions that have the school's guiding principles at the core of every decision they make. This training needs to assist staff in learning to come to consensus so everyone can win. Voting results in winners and losers, leaving losers who will not implement the vision. Additionally, if staff can leave the training clear about who makes what decision and when, they will have the makings of a true shared decision-making structure. This training should also include team building, creating and maintaining a culture that is conducive to change, conducting effective meetings, and delegating responsibility.

After the training, staff must come back to the school and implement what they have learned. The leadership team and the principal are extremely important for keeping the vision at the forefront of everything they do and every decision they make. The job of leaders is to make sure everyone understands their role in implementing the vision and that the vision will, indeed, be implemented. Staff meetings must be about implementing the vision. Grade level and all committee meetings must be about implementing the vision. Time has to be allocated for implementing the vision.

Chapter 9
Partnership Development

Introduction to Partnership Development

The key to effective partnerships—
both partners must contribute,
and both partners must benefit.

Jere Jacobs

Schools that seek to prepare students to live and work in the communication age would do well to establish partnerships with businesses, the community, and parents. These partnerships can make instructional programs exciting and relevant to the purpose of developing all students into successful citizens and quality workers. Partnerships help to reinforce learning at home and may provide solutions to some of the problems teachers face when trying to teach children who are not prepared to learn.

Partnerships can provide schools with information to guide curriculum and instruction, and can help schools to set priorities and achieve goals. Businesses, community groups, and parents are all clients of the school. Involving clients in the continuous improvement of the product—the students—enables schools to make use of talents, resources, and advice from people who have a vested interest.

When establishing a partnership agreement, the organizations lay out goals, and identify desired outcomes and approaches to measuring the success of the partnership. With a comprehensive and detailed strategic plan and the school portfolio, prospective partners can see how they can contribute to the school's larger vision. The key is to let all partners benefit and contribute meaningfully—and celebrate successes, together.

Note. From *The School Portfolio: A Comprehensive Framework for School Improvement,* Second Edition (p.143), by Victoria L. Bernhardt, 1998, Larchmont, NY: Eye on Education. Copyright © 1998 Eye on Education, Inc. Reprinted with permission.

SCHOOL portfolio RTFOLIO

Partnership Development

This Partnership section is organized to add new information each year. The current sections are as follows:

Year One	Year Two	Year Three
• Looking Back on Year One	• Partnership Study Team Vision	• Partnership Implementation Team
• Next Steps	Parent Resource Questionnaire	• Parent-Community Questionnaires
	School Climate Questionnaires	• Health Start
	Parent Education Classes	• Parent Education Classes
	Multicultural Celebration	• Parent Outreach
	After-school Sports Program	• Annual Multicultural Celebration
	Onsite Daycare Program	• Grandparent Reading Program
	Grandparent Reading Program	• Reading Buddies
	Cross-age Tutoring: Reading Buddies	• Watershed Field Work
	School/University Partnership	• Looking Back on Year Three
	Watershed Field Work	• Next Steps
	Health Care	
	• Looking Back on Year Two	
	• Next Steps	

SCHOOL portfolio RTFOLIO

"Parents play one of the most essential roles in the educational process. They provide the environment in which students learn, the discipline and the dedication needed to be successful, not only in school but also in life. Parents must instill in their children a deep respect for hard work, achievement, and learning."

Therese Knecht Dozier

Schools need to help parents understand how to support their children's learning.

Partnership Development

River Road envisions our families, staff, and community working together to help our children succeed. This is a shared responsibility. We are committed to exploring and developing new strategies for our community which will help us and our children meet the challenges of a fast-paced, ever-changing world. Our community will set behavioral and academic standards and be accountable for meeting them.

Present Role of Our Parent Community

River Road parents participate in pre-enrollment orientation meetings with the principal as their children prepare to attend our school. As part of their orientation to the school, parents are invited to complete a parent volunteer form as a way of informing them about school needs and the specific ways in which they can contribute to the school program. New parents are invited to tour the school and to see students and staff in action.

Each fall, all parents and students may attend Back-to-School Night at which time they receive information regarding our PTA and ways in which they can become involved in their child's classroom.

Every six weeks the parent newsletter is mailed to each home. The phone numbers of translators to call for help are printed in each edition. Families needing other language translations are encouraged to call for school news. The newsletter contains information regarding all aspects of the current school program and activities, including a monthly calendar of school events.

Parent volunteers are encouraged to play a vital role in the day-to-day functioning of the school. Parents perform a wide variety of tasks such as fundraising, supporting classroom teachers, chaperoning field trips, helping in the office, preparing the newsletter mailing, etc. Our parent involvement supports fundraisers for science camp, computer/technology donations and purchases, media center materials, and classroom supplies. Thanks to our parents this past year, we have been able to purchase two new computers for our computer lab and have had three others donated.

SCHOOL PORTFOLIO

NOTES

Until partnerships are aligned to the vision of the school, they tend to be lists of work that the school would like the parents to perform.

These are excellent questions defining community involvement that all schools need to ask as they implement effective partnerships.

Even with these efforts, however, the majority of our parents do not become involved in the school. This problem, along with shrinking budgets, changing demographics, and the many different levels of school readiness among our students as evidenced in our demographic data and student achievement scores, is prompting us to rethink the vision for our school. It is also clear that we must develop new strategies for engaging the parent and community support we know is essential for our students' success. In addition, beyond engaging our parent community, we need to explore partnerships with local health care agencies, given the low socioeconomic levels of many of our families and the lack of awareness about health options and regular medical care. We are working with our district to develop a plan of action in this area.

Recognizing that parental involvement is one of the greatest contributors to student success in school, our staff decided to convene a team to develop strategies for increased parent involvement. We have determined, given our community's demographic profile, that we need to provide some well-placed support for our students' families so that they, in turn, can support their children's education. A partnership study team has been convened, and community conversations have been planned for the summer to generate ideas and strategies to involve parents and community members in the development of a new vision and mission for the school. Ultimately, we would like to have a clearly articulated partnership structure for the school, so that our partners' efforts directly impact our students' success in school and in life.

We will develop partnership plans to ensure that our partners have the opportunity to contribute to and benefit from these endeavors. It is our belief that our students have much to give to, as well as learn from, their community. We will look for ways to develop two-way partnerships. However, even from our brief exploration into the concept of Partnership, we are realizing that we need to clarify what we mean by community involvement. The following questions have subsequently arisen:

- How much involvement from community partners is sustainable by our administration and staff?
- How deeply can we realistically weave these partnerships with our curricular goals?
- How do we assure that our partnerships support our students' success and amplify our staff's capacity to deliver a challenging program without burning everyone out?
- What data must we collect to measure whether our partnerships are having an effect on student achievement?

SCHOOL portfolio RTFOLIO

NOTES

The first step in reaching effective partnerships is to make the development of partnerships a part of the school's work. A partnership study team is a good beginning.

Again, tying this element of partnerships back to the vision is extremely important.

Partnership Development—Year One

After our initial data gathering, we began to understand how radically our community's demographics have changed in the past 10 years. Because we hadn't focused on the implications of these data before beginning our school portfolio, we were not effective in our planning nor our dealing with the challenges of a significant number of students and families without cultural literacy skills. Not only did we not have effective strategies for inviting majority parents to participate in the education of their children, we have clearly been unprepared to engage parent partners with cultural backgrounds different from our staff. A partnership study team was formed as a result of the staff's self-assessment using the Education for the Future Initiative Continuous Improvement Continuums. Members of the team include the principal, the office secretary/receptionist, two primary teachers, two upper-grade teachers, our school custodian and two of our most involved parents, one of whom is the assistant manager from our community grocery store /business partner. The first step of the team was to define the scope of their responsibilities.

- Brainstorm strategies for increasing parent and community participation in the school.
- Identify emerging leaders in the parent and business community who would be willing to serve on ongoing school action groups and provide vital perspectives on students' needs and on our change process.
- Develop and evaluate partnerships on the basis of their impact on student learning standards.
- Develop a strategic plan for our partners that will be based on our vision.

Our next task was to mobilize our parent community. An initial brainstorming session resulted in a list of strategies to increase our parents' awareness of the school and the importance of their role in their children's education. Strategies are illustrated in Figure 33 and further discussion follows.

SCHOOL portfolio PORTFOLIO

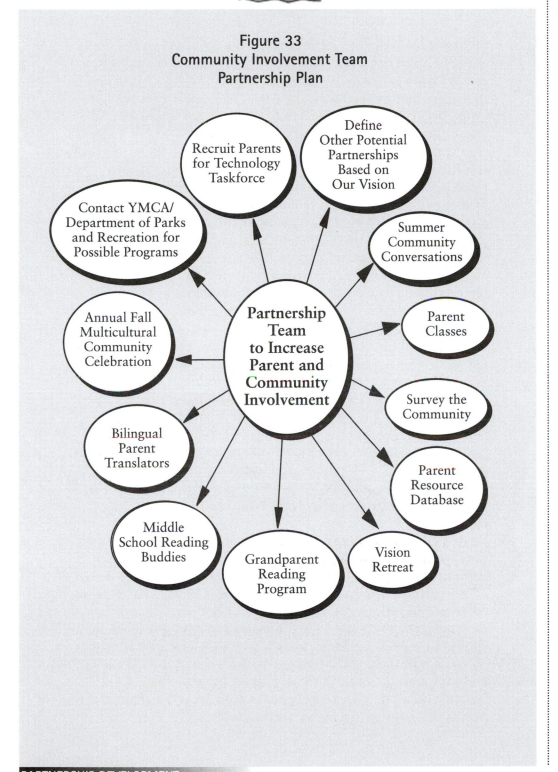

Figure 33
Community Involvement Team
Partnership Plan

Brainstorming all possibilities for inclusive partnerships and developing a plan to serve all aspects of the community and vision is important.

SCHOOL **portfolio** PORTFOLIO

One of the real benefits of the school portfolio is the public documentation of the plans for implementing the vision, and in this case, including and effectively involving and listening to parents and the community.

- Hold informal, summer gatherings, "Community Conversations" at the home of one of our parents with discussions centering around what parents want for their children. Our goal is to engage parents in thoughtful discussions about education, to seek their input, hear their concerns and to help them understand the importance of their involvement in the school. We feel that this is a strategy we can begin implementing immediately with our English-speaking families, but we envision similar gatherings for our Hmong families where the family/school disconnect is greatest. This could become a vital avenue for communicating the importance of education for their children and would also help us develop a better understanding of the Hmong culture. Through this kind of "grass-roots" conversation, we would be able to better assess the needs of our students and their families. This understanding would allow us to build powerful, high-impact partnerships.

- To support the above effort and to make school gatherings, meetings, and conferences accessible to all our parents, we would like to develop a small core of bilingual parent translators who would be willing to contact non-English-speaking families and translate for them. We are also considering having these bilingual parents facilitate key meetings in our non-English speaking families' native languages, so that the awkwardness of the translation process is eliminated. Further exploration and dialogue are planned to pinpoint the most effective strategy for identifying and training these parents. We are hoping to earmark some Title 1 funds so that our community translators can be paid for their efforts.

- Have a fall school vision retreat with staff, parent, and community business partners involved in the shaping of the new vision and mission of the school. This would help us develop a clear purpose of our partnerships, and then would allow us to align partnership outcomes and structures with our vision.

- Develop a parent resource questionnaire and database so we know where our parents work, what interests and talents they have that they might be willing to contribute to the work of the school, and what volunteer areas might be of interest to them. Have these resource questionnaires be assigned as homework for the students to ensure we get the return we need.

SCHOOL **portfolio** RTFOLIO

Data can help with the effective implementation of partnerships and the vision.

Effective partnership programs include what the school can do for the partners.

Win-win partnerships are the ideal.

- Develop schoolwide perception questionnaires to seek input from all parents, staff, and students so we know how everyone is experiencing River Road. We need to be able to disaggregate and chart these data so we have a clear picture of our school's strengths as well as areas needing improvement. As part of the parent questionnaire, an open-ended question would be included to find out whether parents would be interested in parent education classes, and, if so, what subjects would be of greatest interest to them.
- Develop adult education classes to support identified needs of our families (determined from school questionnaires), such as:
  * English/Cultural Literacy
  * Technology Training
  * Parent Education
  * Family Math
- Start an annual school multicultural community celebration to raise community awareness about and to celebrate our cultural diversity. Consider inviting local businesses. There is much we do not know about each other and an event of this kind can begin to establish the climate of belonging we believe is important for our students.
- Develop a grandparent reading program. Contact nearby retirement community to solicit volunteers to read with students needing individual reading support for two hours per week. Be able to track the impact of this support program on student achievement.
- Develop a cross-age reading buddies tutoring program with our feeder middle school.
- Recruit parents for a technology task force. While this will primarily be a staff-led committee, we are hoping that a couple of our parents with expertise in this area could be valuable contributors to the school's overall technology plan.
- Define other partnerships we might want to develop to support our vision, such as health care services and the involvement of our city council with our school and community issues. It is also important that we develop a listing of local businesses and consider how we might ask for their support and/or direct involvement with the school.

SCHOOL **portfolio** RTFOLIO

- Build partnerships with local agencies to target areas of community and family concern such as alcohol/substance abuse, family violence and food/shelter needs.
- Work with the city's Parks and Recreation Department to establish an onsite afterschool sports program.
- Work with the YMCA to establish an onsite, afterschool daycare program.

Looking Back on Year One

We realized that there was a wealth of partnership opportunities that we had never considered. This team's work has the potential to change the school in very dramatic, positive ways. We are a little overwhelmed at the scope of our brainstorming list, however. Our primary resource is time, and we must make efficient and clear use of our own time as well as the time of parents and community partners we ask to become involved in the River Road school community. We were so enthusiastic about our ideas that we wanted to start everything moving at once! We prioritized our recommendations and presented them to the leadership team for feedback and approval. Our success will depend a great deal on the alignment of all our efforts and the quality of our communication to everyone.

Next Steps

- We need to define our overall partnership outcomes, structure, and process.
- We need to define our student learning outcomes to know how best to include partners.
- We need to establish a strategic plan for partners related to our vision and involve everyone in the planning process.
- We need to be clear on what we mean by and want for family involvement in order to increase parent participation in student learning.

SCHOOL **portfolio** RTFOLIO

Partnership Development—Year Two

Partnership Study Team

After our partnership team presented our brainstorming strategies and received faculty input and approval in June, we were able to prioritize our efforts. With the added parent support and enthusiasm of our summer meetings, however, we are discovering that we can tackle much more than we originally thought possible. This team is now part of our overall leadership/study team group, and one of our parents will be on the leadership team. As part of researching how best to implement a new partnership vision for the school, we are charged with—

- creating opportunities for parents and community partners to get involved with the school in meaningful ways
- supporting parents to support their children's learning at home
- finding ways to coordinate with social services, health agencies, and other community resources (including resources to support hands-on learning)

Using the values and beliefs statement generated at the retreat, we have revisited our partnership brainstorming ideas and have made sure they are congruent with our vision for the school. The following activities have been undertaken with the guidance of the partnership study team:

Vision

By the end of the summer a strong, committed group of 30 parents were ready to meet with faculty. Based on our community conversations and the partnership study team's brainstorming list, several parents have volunteered to follow through on key goals. They have agreed to join the partnership study team, allowing us to keep our efforts clearly focused. These community members were also invited to participate in the fall vision retreat. As the retreat progressed, it was energizing for everyone to realize that the emerging vision was highly congruent with the vision parents had begun describing over the summer. The creation of this shared vision has become a strong, unifying force for the entire community. The vision statement that resulted from the retreat is providing a solid foundation and inspiration for our partnership efforts.

The vision must be at the center of partnerships.

Parent questionnaires are helpful in understanding parents' perceptions of the learning environment. It is not easy to develop an effective parent questionnaire. Use help whenever it is available and pilot the questionnaire.

River Road Elementary School Vision Statement

…Our families, staff and community will work together to nurture and develop a deep appreciation for each other's cultures. The entire River Road School community will feel welcomed and appreciated at our school. Working in partnership with parents and community, we will ensure that individual student needs, gifts, and learning styles are respected and addressed. Students will leave River Road ready for future learning.

Parent Resource Questionnaire

River Road Value: Educating students is a shared responsibility
A parent resource questionnaire (see Figure 34) and introductory letter was developed and sent home with our students as a homework assignment for their parents. One of our parents designed the questionnaire and database so we could create a resource binder as well as having the sorting power of a database. With the help of this database, we are now able to identify volunteer translators and have begun to define the role of the bilingual volunteer translators. The partnership task force members are familiarizing themselves with the resources identified through the questionnaire and are looking at how this information can be systematically used to support the school's goals.

School Climate Questionnaires

River Road Value: Educating students is a shared responsibility
School climate questionnaires, using Education for the Future Initiative's templates, were administered last March to parents, students and staff. Their results were charted and studied by the staff. The student and staff survey responses are being used in combination with student achievement data and school processes information, and provide us with valuable perception data. The results are reported in our Information and Analysis section. Our parent survey information was sketchy, however. We surveyed parents at Back-to-School Night, but due to the low numbers of parents who attended, our information is not reflective of the entire parent community. The questionnaire return from our Hmong families was especially poor. The language and cultural barrier is something we clearly need to address. We are rethinking our strategy for surveying parents next year.

SCHOOL portfolio PORTFOLIO

Figure 34
RIVER ROAD PARENT RESOURCE QUESTIONNAIRE

Parent Information:		Children:		
Name:			Name	Grade	School
Address:		1)			
City:	Zip:	2)			
Phone (hm):		3)			
Phone (wk):		4)			
Fax		5)			
E-mail:		6)			
Best time to call:					

What skills, interests, hobbies, or talents do you have which you would be willing to share with the River Road community? Please check all that apply.

❑ Carpentry   ❑ Landscaping   ❑ Videotaping   ❑ Web Page Design
❑ Word Processing   ❑ Technology   ❑ Literature   ❑ Wallpapering
❑ Sewing Costumes   ❑ Telephoning   ❑ Tutoring   ❑ Fundraising
❑ Page Layout/Graphics ❑ Gardening   ❑ Photography   ❑ _____
❑ _____   ❑ _____   ❑ _____   ❑ _____

Do you belong to a company or any community organizations that might be willing to donate any of the following? Please check and describe all that apply.

❑ Materials _____   ❑ Services _____
❑ Resources _____   ❑ Funding _____

Would your employer be interested in a mutually beneficial community partnership? Yes ❑

Does your employer have a matching grant program? Yes ❑

Does your employer have a support/donation program that might be beneficial to our students?

    Yes ❑ *Short description:* _____

Company Info:	Company Name:		Phone:
	Address:		Contact
	City:	Zip:	Person:

Do you have any special life experiences which you would be willing to share with our students?

    Yes ❑ *Short description:* _____

Do you speak languages other than English? Yes ❑ _____

Would you be willing to volunteer to support River Road students, or do you know a ❑ neighbor, ❑ friend, ❑ relative, or ❑ retiree, who would be interested? What would you or they be interested in doing? _____

If you are already involved at River Road, in what capacity? ❑ _____
❑ _____   ❑ _____   ❑ _____

Would you like more information regarding the different volunteer groups at River Road? Yes ❑

NOTES

Some mechanism for understanding how parents can contribute is needed. They may not speak up otherwise.

SCHOOL **portfolio** PORTFOLIO

Parent Education Classes

River Road Value: Meeting basic needs, working together to support families and students

The following classes are in the developmental stages based on parent interest:

- A parent/teacher team model is being considered to teach technology classes. Introductory Claris Works classes will be taught.
- Three faculty members are collaborating to present a family math evening as a way of bringing families onto campus and supporting family involvement in student learning.
- One of our language specialists will prepare an evening class for English language learners.
- A community marriage and family therapist has been contacted to teach a parenting skills class.
- Our local police officers association will provide a drug education program for students, and will present information at a parent education night.

SCHOOL portfolio PORTFOLIO

NOTES

Schools must include ways to celebrate the cultural heritages of all the families. Diversity of the community needs to be imbedded in both school events and in the curriculum.

Multicultural Celebration

River Road Value: Valuing the cultures and customs of our families

We hosted our first annual multicultural celebration/community potluck in October. A group of dedicated parent volunteers began planning this event as part of the summer conversations. They called all the families in the school and invited them to the gathering. Local businesses were also invited to attend. It was the largest turnout in recent history, and it is the first time many of our Hmong families have participated in a school event. Families brought traditional foods and we invited them to bring things to share their cultural heritage. One of the ice-breaking activities was to have each family draw on a paper flag something about their country of origin. Each family then came forward and spoke about their flags and whatever they'd brought to share. We taped each flag to the wall outside our cafeteria so that we all could see and celebrate who we are as a community. There were warm feelings all around, and some tearful moments. Our Hmong families

YEAR TWO

SCHOOL portfolio RTFOLIO

NOTES

In the school's approach to supporting families' lives and the school vision, include all ages and aspects of the day (i.e., before school, during school, after school, and pre-school-age children).

brought many pieces of their wonderful embroidery. Their story quilts were especially powerful in helping everyone understand their journey from Laos through refugee camps to the U.S. We are hoping to have a lobby display of their artwork later this year. Our principal gave a short (translated) talk about the school's vision and invited parents to get involved in a school activity or class that interested them. There is new energy and enthusiasm pervading the school as a result of the vision retreat and this community event.

After-school Sports Program

River Road Value: Supporting varied needs and learning styles of children as well as meeting basic needs of families

The Parks and Recreation Department began a well-received after-school sports program using our outside space and our cafeteria. Although this program is available for students throughout the city, its on-campus location makes it especially attractive for River Road students.

Onsite Daycare Program

River Road Value: Meeting basic needs, working together to support families and students

The YMCA will begin an onsite after-school daycare program in January. They will share space with the kindergarten classrooms.

SCHOOL PORTFOLIO

Grandparent Reading Program

River Road Value: Literacy

Development of the grandparent reading program has begun to support our literacy focus. Local retirement community volunteers are being recruited and trained on our standards so everyone shares common goals. They will read with students needing individual reading support for two hours per week. Ideally, as our database is developed, we plan to flag the students who participate in this program and use our pre/post standardized test scores and running records to measure student achievement increases in reading. This will help us determine the impact of this support program on student achievement.

Cross-age Tutoring: Reading Buddies

River Road Value: Literacy

In tandem with the grandparent reading program, we have approached our nearby middle school, River Glen Middle School, to recruit students for a cross-age tutoring program to provide additional support to our below-grade-level students. We plan to have eight to ten students each semester working one-on-one as reading buddies with third and grade four students. They will be trained in a program that helps below-grade-level readers to achieve grade-level standards. Both these programs will help our efforts to improve grade three reading scores.

School/University Partnership

River Road Value: Hands-on curriculum development, standards development

The staff began a partnership with our nearby university's agricultural extension for training and professional development to help us implement the Adopt-a-Watershed curriculum. Staff participation is voluntary at this point. We will assess the effectiveness of this program at the end of this year. (See Professional Development.)

Watershed Field Work

River Road Value: Hands-on curriculum development

As part of River Road's hands-on emphasis and work with the Adopt-A-Watershed curriculum, our team has contacted the city's environmental planning agency to see how we might develop some

SCHOOL **portfolio** RTFOLIO

When basic needs of children are met through school-community partnerships, teachers can spend more time in classrooms focusing on the learning needs of children.

Measuring the impact of the partnerships can help the school know what and how to improve in the area of partnerships.

hands-on, service learning projects for our students. The agency is receptive to our request, and meetings with our team representative who has volunteered to head up these efforts are underway. We are doing fieldwork in the local watershed with the city's environmental planning group. Students are involved in water-testing and reforestation projects.

Health Care

River Road Value: Meeting basic needs

Two partnership team members and the district's school health nurse are working with local social service and health care agencies to begin the application process for a Healthy Start grant to support our many families who are unable to provide basic health care for their children. They plan to submit the grant proposal in the fall. We should hear whether we qualify next spring.

Looking Back on Year Two

This has been an exciting year! Much has been undertaken with the support of so many of our partners, and our partnerships have brought more resources to the school than we imagined possible a year ago. We need to stay focused on continuing the activities that have been such a big "win" for the school—especially the multicultural celebration. Our core team of parents who created this event are documenting their steps. Their priority will be to recruit others this year to maintain the long-term sustainability. Since we already have so many of our projects underway, our team members have chosen to make the transition from the study team to the implementation team.

Next Steps

- We must implement a systematic and systemic way to measure the impact of our partnerships on student achievement.
- We need to make sure our parent, community, and business partnerships are used throughout the school and organized in a way that clearly supports our vision for River Road students.
- We need to make sure that all of our partners are feeling appreciated and see the results of their work with our students.

SCHOOL portfolio RTFOLIO

Partnership Development—Year Three

Partnership Implementation Team

The team continues to meet monthly to monitor progress on our partnerships. We continue to use our questionnaire data to self-assess our work and to see if new issues or needs are arising in the community. All partnerships and community development work continue to move forward, although sustaining the efforts at involving non-English-speaking families is challenging as volunteers come and go. There is a tendency for the same parents to be involved in everything. It is essential for the sustainability of our parent and community involvement that we make a concerted effort each year to recruit new members for the partnership team. It is clear that outreach is everything! The main job (and challenge!) of the partnership implementation team is communication. We have discovered that as time consuming as they are, the one-on-one phone calls and face-to-face conversations we have initiated are the most effective means of communication we have. They have yielded the greatest turnouts at school events.

UPDATE ON...
PARTNERSHIP

THE RIVER ROAD VISION RETREAT WAS A HUGE SUCCESS! POSTERS WITH OUR NEW VISION ARE BEING MADE AND WILL BE READY FOR YOU TO POST IN YOUR ROOMS BEFORE THANKSGIVING. THANKS FOR AN **INSPIRING** GATHERNG...

OTHER PARTNERSHIP NEWS....

1. **Climate Surveys** have been scheduled for the first week in February. Check your boxes for regular progress reports and updates!

2. Our **Adopt-A-Watershed** partnership has begun at River Road (see photos at left). Contact Nancy and Donna for additional information, hands-on science units, and classroom field trips to test water quality at the river.

3. We are in conversation with the Senior Center about starting a **Grandparent Reading Program.** We will be asking each teacher for a list of students who would benefit from one-on-one tutoring with a caring elder. Look for ongoing info in your boxes.

4. The **Parent Resource Questionnaire** Update: Parent volunteer, Janice Olsewski, is compiling our database of parent skills and interests. More to follow on this one... we have a wealth of resources right here at home!

We need to continually revisit our purposes as a group to keep our priorities clear. Our leadership team representative keeps us informed about the progress of the other implementation teams, and we all regularly check the staff room posters to see how everyone is progressing. Our yearly school self-assessment allows us to make sure our efforts are integrated with all other school systems. More importantly, it helps us stay focused on our vision.

SCHOOL portfolio PORTFOLIO

Parent Community Questionnaires

Our questionnaires have been updated and administered. Communication around data continues to be strong so that staff and community are using data effectively to evaluate our progress. We have found our parent, student, and staff questionnaires used in combination with our student achievement data to be a helpful tool in assessing our progress toward our vision.

Healthy Start

To our great delight, we were awarded the Healthy Start grant we applied for last year. As a result, we have been able to open an onsite children's health clinic, and have begun to coordinate other parent health education and counseling services for our families through the clinic. The city's family counseling clinic, which provides support for students and families in our district, now holds individual, family and group counseling sessions onsite. One of the side benefits of this clinic is that the number of families who are on campus have dramatically increased—especially our low income families who have been our most difficult population to reach. With the advent of the clinic and activities such as our multicultural celebration, it is clear that our school is becoming a place where all families feel welcome. As parents come to the clinic for appointments, they now often drop into their child's classroom to observe or to help. While this has been challenging at times for the teachers, all are in agreement that the benefits of the increased family involvement and comfort level are beginning to be seen in our student's school preparation and attendance.

Parent Education Classes

Classes were offered in parenting skills, English language development, and beginning word processing training. A very successful, first family math evening provided yet another way for parents to feel a vital part of their child's education.

Parent Outreach

We continue to reach our parents using our most effective means of rallying parents to important school events: face-to-face contact at school, our phone

SCHOOL portfolio PORTFOLIO

Evaluating partnerships includes:

- *Asking partners if they feel they are contributing*
- *Asking students about their perspective of the impact of the partnership*
- *Looking at the student achievement results in the areas of the partnerships*

tree, and backpack mail. We are investigating purchasing software that would allow the school to program call-outs to our families to keep them apprised of current events. With the health care clinic on campus, we have had more opportunities to reach out to families who don't usually participate in the school. It is slow going, but we are encouraged that we've been able to recruit two more translators for our Hmong families. These efforts combined with onsite childcare in the evenings and on Saturdays are gradually bringing more of our Hmong families to school meetings and events.

Annual Multicultural Celebration

This event is becoming the heart of our school's culture. A strong parent committee continues to organize this event and some of the parents are now working with teachers to include more culturally relevant activities in the classroom. The committee has been considering expanding this event to include a walk-a-thon fundraiser, and has plans to visit a neighboring county's elementary school which has successfully been running this type of fundraising event for the past five years. It has become both a profitable and efficient way to raise money for the school as well

SCHOOL PORTFOLIO

as a wonderful community-strengthening event. We'd like to create something similar, and use the talents of our Hmong artists to help in creating a River Road story quilt as our first walk-a-thon theme that will show how all our families arrived at this community.

Grandparent Reading Program

A description of the partnership plan with our retirement community has been completed and is posted in their community center as well as in our office. Our Reading Recovery teachers have trained our grandparent volunteers in how to support childrens' reading efforts. The evaluation of the effectiveness of our volunteers' efforts has shown increases in student reading levels. The success of this program has encouraged us to add an additional oral history component. Students at all grade levels will interview the seniors about their lives and document their stories in writing. A book of the oral history of the town will be compiled and an evening of storytelling, including a reception for all the authors, will be the culminating event.

Reading Buddies

The cross-age tutoring program established with our nearby middle school is yielding some wonderful results. Our students look up to their middle school tutors, our middle school students (often graduates of River Road) are gaining valuable community service experience, and this additional classroom literacy support is also supporting reading gains for our below-grade-level readers. Everyone wins in this partnership.

Watershed Field Work

As part of River Road's hands-on emphasis and work with the Adopt-A-Watershed curriculum, our students are doing fieldwork in the local watershed with the city's environmental planning group. Students from the four classes where teachers have been trained are involved in water-testing and reforestation and study projects using the native grasses along our river. Parents have enthusiastically turned out to support the field trips, and the participating teachers have been sharing their activities with the rest of the staff. The idea of

SCHOOL **portfolio** RTFOLIO

combining a strong, hands-on science curriculum focus (and tying in math, reading, and writing skills) with the service learning component of Adopt-A-Watershed is finally catching hold among the staff. Two parents have requested to be included in the staff training at the summer institute. This partnership will allow our parent resources to support this growing program.

Looking Back on Year Three

As our partnerships grow and require further elaboration, we are finding that we have fewer resources (time and people) to explore additional partnerships that might be of benefit to our students. It takes more energy and people to fully implement our programs as they grow! Our primary concern is to stay focused on our vision and to make sure that the partnerships we undertake are maintained well and are satisfactory relationships for everyone. We know that we would like to broach a partnership with the local technology manufacturer, but have not been able to identify a parent/partnership liaison to head up those efforts. Our staff technology resource teacher will make inquiries this summer. We are hoping our parent resource database will help us locate a parent who is an employee of the company and would be willing to be the primary contact. As our networking infrastructure becomes more complex, it would be helpful to have some knowledgeable input from professionals.

Overall, though, when we look at where we were three years ago, we have made substantial progress in creating community partnerships that are helping us to make the River Road vision a reality.

SCHOOL portfolio PORTFOLIO

Next Steps:

- We have earnestly begun to recruit new task force members so that a shared history of our partnership efforts is maintained. It is our recommendation that the leadership of this group must always include the principal, however, staff, parent, and community members may rotate. One of our core parent partners who has been instrumental in helping to develop and sustain our grandparent reading program and our reading buddies program is "graduating" this year and we need to make sure we have someone who can step into that liaison position.
- We must make sure that we are connecting to all the possible partners in our community that make sense for our students' learning.
- We will formalize our partners' efforts and our successes with an awards dinner and a plaque at the end of each school year.

Partnership Development Summary
from the Authors' Perspectives

River Road made a substantial shift in their engagement and use of parent and community partnerships during these three years. The initial development of a shared vision at the vision retreat was the first and most crucial step in the formulation of a clear partnership strategy. As staff and involved parents and community partners focused on student learning objectives, there were obvious unmet needs that could be met through planned community involvement. A partnership plan was developed and clear goals were established. Team members volunteered to assume leadership for different aspects of the plan. The Continuous Improvement Continuums and the community involvement team's partnership plan are used as the framework for monitoring progress and setting goals.

Items for the Partnership Development Section

The Partnership Development section of your school portfolio is where staff describe their partnerships with businesses, the community, parents, and higher education. Items that might go in this section of your school portfolio include—

- Assessments on the Education for the Future Initiative Partnership Development Continuous Improvement Continuum (River Road's appears in the Continuous Improvement and Evaluation section of their school portfolio)
- Analysis of what needs to happen to move to the next steps in the continuum
- Description of why your school wants partnerships and what all partners will get out of the relationship
- How business, parents, and community partnerships can help the school and support student learning goals
- School partnership plan
- Descriptions of *current* parent, community, and business involvement with the school
- Descriptions of *desired* parent, community, and business involvement with the school
- Evidence of partnerships' impact on increasing student learning and attendance, and decreasing absenteeism, drop-out rates, etc.
- Evaluation of the impact of the partnerships on the school and the partners
- Descriptions of what the partners got out of the partnership
- Goals for improvement

Making the Difference for Partnership Development Continuous Improvement

In addition to ensuring that all parties contribute and all parties benefit, the key to effective partnership development is to build relationships that will help with the implementation of the vision.

Partnerships can help align all the parts of the learning organization. Based on the population of the school, specific communities are encouraged to participate to ensure inclusion and understanding, and to build relationships. With the inclusion of all aspects of the community, a vision that works for all children can be implemented. As Margaret Wheatley says, "Power in organizations is the capacity generated by relationships."

Recommendations

Everyone wants to support schools. We just need to know how to get involved, how our contributions will be used, and that these contributions will have lasting impact. When partnership involvement is tied to the vision and school plan, partners can see how they contribute to the bigger picture of the school, and know that their contributions add value.

A School Portfolio provides excellent documentation for partners in understanding what the school is about and how their contributions have assisted with the implementation of the vision. Often with this type of documentation, partners can see ways to contribute that the school did not see.

Steps to establishing a partnership development plan might include the following:
1. Determine, as a staff, reasons for and preferences of types of partnerships.
2. Create a study team to coordinate and plan for partnerships.
3. Study team investigates how partnerships can help the school staff achieve student learning standards and their school improvement goals:
   - Visit other schools with successful partnerships
   - Read research
   - Brainstorm areas in which partnerships will benefit students
4. Partnership team creates plan for partnerships at the school and submits plan and rationale to staff for discussion.
5. Staff adds to and approves partnership plan.
6. Partnership team contacts prospective partners to determine interest.

7. Interested prospective partners meet with partnership team to exchange information about interests, and to learn about each other's organizations:
   - Prospective partners describe why they want a partnership with the school and how they would like it to continue
   - Partnership team utilizes school portfolio to describe the school's mission, vision, values and beliefs, student learning standards, and current operations and processes
8. Partners prepare an agreement, establish outcomes, and determine how the partnership will be monitored and improved on a continuous basis:
   - Regular meeting times are established
   - Cost and personnel requirements for the partnership are identified
   - Celebrate and thank the partners for their contributions

Chapter 10
Continuous
Improvement
and Evaluation

Introduction to
Continuous Improvement and Evaluation

Continuous Improvement causes us to
think about upstream process improvement,
not downstream damage control.

Teams and Tools

Continuous improvement and evaluation is the process of assessing plans, implementation, processes, and progress to determine what needs to improve and how to make those improvements. The assessment and improvement steps are then repeated on an ongoing basis. These principles have been used successfully in the corporate world for many years and can be used successfully in the school improvement process as well.

Note. From *The School Portfolio: A Comprehensive Framework for School Improvement,* Second Edition (p.161), by Victoria L. Bernhardt, 1998, Larchmont, NY: Eye on Education. Copyright © 1998 Eye on Education, Inc. Reprinted with permission.

SCHOOL portfolio PORTFOLIO

Continuous Improvement and Evaluation

This Continuous Improvement and Evaluation section is organized to add new information each year. The current sections are as follows:

Year One	Year Two	Year Three
• Continuous Improvement Continuums (CICs) Assessment Baseline	• CICs Assessment	• CIC Assessment
• Summary and Next Steps	• Summary and Next Steps	• Summary and Next Steps

Before embarking on any serious self-assessment, the school must establish a positive tone and a safe environment. Clarify ground rules and meeting etiquette, such as—

GROUND RULES EXAMPLE

- *This is a safe room*
- *There is no rank in this room*
- *All ideas are valid*
- *Each person gets a chance to speak*
- *Each person gets a chance to listen*
- *What we decide here, everyone will implement*
- *We are here to focus on the future*
- *Our purpose is improvement, not blame*

YEAR ONE

SCHOOL portfolio PORTFOLIO

MEETING ETIQUETTE EXAMPLE

- *Raise your hand and be recognized before speaking*
- *Be brief and to the point*
- *Make your point calmly*
- *Keep an open mind*
- *Listen without bias*
- *Understand what is said*
- *Avoid side conversations*
- *Respect other opinions*
- *Avoid personal agendas*
- *Come prepared to do what is good for the organization*
- *Have fun*

River Road Elementary School
Continuous Improvement Continuums Assessment Baseline

In the spring of year one, River Road staff conducted a baseline assessment of our school on the Education for the Future Initiative Continuous Improvement Continuums. Each staff member made her/his personal rating. Staff members discussed why they thought the school was where they rated it. The staff came to consensus on a number that represented where the entire school was for each of the sections. The ratings and brief discussions for each Continuum follow.

SCHOOL portfolio RTFOLIO

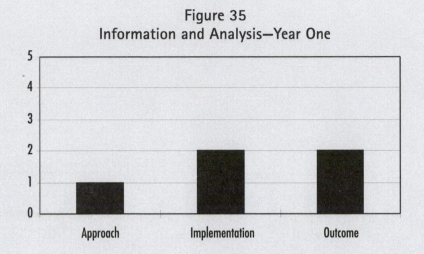

Figure 35
Information and Analysis—Year One

Information and Analysis

Collectively, staff felt that River Road was a 1 in Approach, 2 in Implementation, and 2 in Outcome with respect to Information and Analysis. Data are currently not gathered in any systematic way. Standardized student achievement scores are only available in paper form, except for special programs. Some data are tracked for special programs because it is required of the district. Teachers of these special programs, i.e., English as a Second Language, Title 1, and Reading Recovery track the data for River Road; therefore, change, based on data, is only limited to those areas. The district gathers more data, but does not typically share the data with the schools.

Next Steps:

- We need to gather and utilize multiple measures of data systematically on a schoolwide basis, and look at all K-5 data to get to the root causes of problems and to understand what we need to improve.
- We need to administer and analyze questionnaire data for students, teachers, and parents to understand our clients' perceptions and needs, and to compile resulting charts in an interpreted, organized way in our school portfolio.
- We need to build the capacity of individuals in the school and at the district level to do the data analysis work.

SCHOOL **portfolio** RTFOLIO

NOTES

It is important to have staff members make their individual ratings before sharing and coming to consensus as a group. This is how schools are able to know real perceptions of members of their staff. (See Appendix A for instructions on using the Continuous Improvement Continuums.)

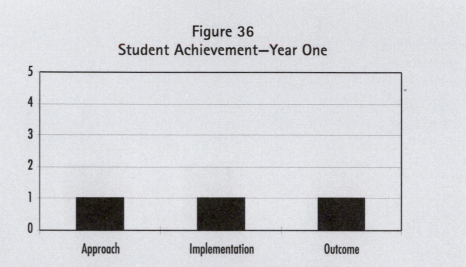

Figure 36
Student Achievement—Year One

Student Achievement

River Road staff rated the school a 1 in Approach with respect to Student Achievement, 1 in Implementation, and 1 in Outcome, largely because neither the school nor district have identified learning standards for students, although the district is currently in the process of developing language arts standards. Staff feel that instructional and organizational processes critical to student success have not been identified, and student achievement trends are not being tracked or analyzed schoolwide. There is also a feeling that some teachers believe that not all students can achieve, and that student backgrounds are often used as an excuse for low student achievement. However, with the little data available, some teachers in special programs are understanding how to fill the learning gaps of students.

Next Steps:

- We need to identify standards for student learning at the school level, with representative input. The process used will be very important.
- We need to get serious about authentic assessment.
- We need to increase communication across and within grade levels for a continuum of learning that makes sense for students.
- We need data in a form other than paper to inform our work.
- We need to create a clear vision that is shared by all staff and not just teachers.

SCHOOL **portfolio** RTFOLIO

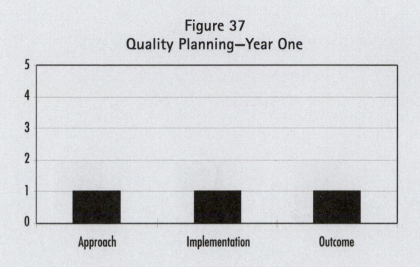

Figure 37
Quality Planning—Year One

Approach   Implementation   Outcome

NOTES

Do not worry about low ratings. If established as an honest process, the low ratings will motivate staff. Be honest about where the school is right now. The important thing is to do something to get higher ratings before the next assessment.

Quality Planning

River Road staff rated the school a 1 in Approach, 1 in Implementation, and 1 in Outcome for Quality Planning. Currently, there are many plans for the school. We have a technology plan, a professional development plan, a schoolwide improvement plan, a Title 1 plan, and an English language development plan. Staff work is carried out in isolation, and the principal keeps the budget.

Next Steps:

- We need to revisit our vision and then develop one plan that is consistent with the vision. We need to look at and analyze data to inform the plan.
- We need to apply for schoolwide funding using our school plan in order to utilize Title 1 funds for all students.
- We need to include teachers, administrators, parents, and students in the planning process and make sure everyone owns it.
- We need to budget money based on the plan.
- We need to revisit our mission statement to involve everyone in the school in developing and owning the statement. We need to identify values and beliefs and the purpose of the school in order to create the mission.

SCHOOL portfolio RTFOLIO

NOTES

When coming to agreement on a number that represents where the school is on the Continuous Improvement Continuums, do not average the staff's ratings. An average reduces the ownership to a number and decreases the sense of urgency to improve.

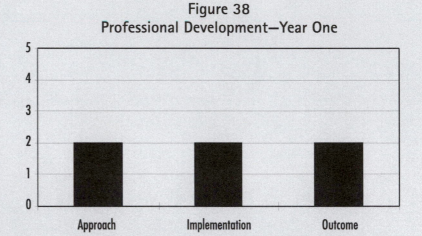

Figure 38
Professional Development—Year One

Professional Development

River Road staff assessed the school on Professional Development as a 2 in Approach, 2 in Implementation, and 2 in Outcome. Staff have been able to choose the professional development they want to attend without regard to an overall school plan. Therefore, professional development has been unfocused and lacking in what is needed schoolwide. Additionally, we have not analyzed the effectiveness of our professional development efforts.

Next Steps:

• We need to clarify our professional development needs schoolwide.
• We need to plan for professional development related to our vision, our overall school plan and the results we are getting, and stop our cafeteria approach to professional development.
• Our future professional development activities need to be planned in advance, include and involve all staff, and be ongoing.
• We have to clarify our vision, mission, and student learning standards before we can go any farther.

SCHOOL **portfolio** PORTFOLIO

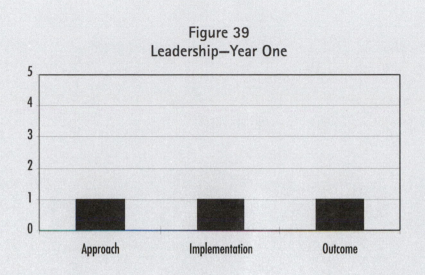

Figure 39
Leadership—Year One

Leadership

Staff felt that River Road was a 1 in Approach, 1 in Implementation, and 1 in Outcome with respect to school Leadership. River Road is attempting to implement shared decision-making, although staff needs to define what we mean by shared decision-making before it can be successful. Currently, the principal makes all decisions with little or no input from others. The decisions lack consistency with little staff buy-in.

Next Steps:

- We need to clarify a leadership structure for the school that respects and is acceptable to all individuals in the school.
- We need to continue to improve our communication structure to keep everyone informed and to ensure that principal and teacher participation and input are sought and used.
- Teachers and staff need to feel that the school "includes" them and does not just "do" to them. Clarifying the school values and beliefs, the purpose of the school, mission, vision, and student learning standards will help considerably.

SCHOOL portfolio RTFOLIO

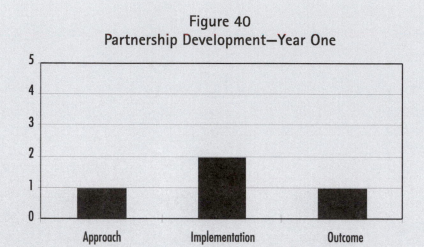

**Figure 40
Partnership Development—Year One**

Partnership Development

Staff rated the school a 1 in Approach, 2 in Implementation, and 1 in Outcome with regard to Partnership Development. There is no real system for input from parents, business, or community, although a group of teachers has been seeking effective community/business partnerships and effective parent involvement. Teachers now feel that a plan for gaining parent and community partnerships is needed for schoolwide implementation.

Next Steps:

- We need to define our overall partnership outcomes, structure, and process.
- We need to define our student learning standards to know how best to include partners.
- We need to define a strategic plan for partners related to our vision and involve parents, businesses, and the community in the planning.
- We need to work on what we mean by, and want for, family involvement in order to increase participation.

SCHOOL portfolio RTFOLIO

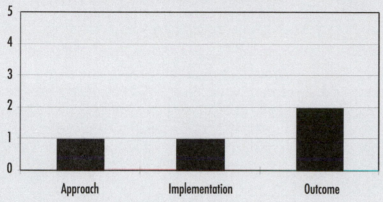

Figure 41
Continuous Improvement and Evaluation—Year One

NOTES
These discussions allow everyone to know what is going on at the school and what is possible.

Continuous Improvement and Evaluation

With respect to the big picture, Continuous Improvement and Evaluation, staff rated the school a 1 in Approach, 1 in Implementation, and 2 in Outcome. Currently, there are neither strategies nor plans for continuous improvement and evaluation. Individual teachers or the principal change things only when something sparks the need to improve. Decisions are reactive and problems are solved temporarily.

If we continue along the path we started this week, we will soon get to preventative and proactive work.

Next Steps:

- We need to see accomplishments for the year.
- We need a way to evaluate and analyze everything that we do.
- We need to continue looking at the big picture of the school and how to continuously improve all parts of the organization.
- We need and want a cooperative system for change with a communication structure that will keep everyone apprised of what is going on.

SCHOOL **portfolio** PORTFOLIO

NOTES

Using this process, staff realize they cannot intelligently change anything they do until they have data. Staff also discover that their guiding principles, i.e., vision, mission, and purpose based on the values and beliefs of staff, are they key to everything they do. They must clarify their guiding principles or they can go no farther.

Summary and Next Steps
Continuous Improvement Continuum Baseline
Year One

Members of the River Road Elementary School staff conducted a baseline assessment on each of the Education for the Future Initiative Continuous Improvement Continuums. Staff made their personal rating of where they thought the school was on each continuum, and then everyone agreed upon one number that represented where they as a group felt the school was. Next steps were developed for each continuum. The overall next steps in priority order are shown below.

Overall Next Steps:

- We need to build a comprehensive and systematic data analysis system for our continuous improvement. We can start by creating and administering questionnaires for our students, teachers, and parents in order to understand their perceptions of the learning environment and their needs, and by charting our student achievement data.
- We need to work with the district to help define all our student learning standards.
- We need to revisit our mission and vision via staff values and beliefs and the purpose of the school. We then need to create a comprehensive schoolwide plan—an overall plan that includes student achievement, professional development, leadership, and partnership development.
- We need to create a shared decision-making structure that is congruent with the vision of the school.
- We need to include our parent, community, and business partners in an effective manner in everything that we do.

CONTINUOUS IMPROVEMENT

SCHOOL portfolio RTFOLIO

River Road Elementary School
Continuous Improvement Continuums Assessment
Year Two

Figure 42
Information and Analysis—Year Two

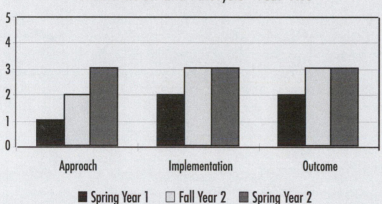

■ Spring Year 1   □ Fall Year 2   ■ Spring Year 2

Information and Analysis

Collectively, staff felt that by the fall of year two, River Road had moved from a 1 in Approach, 2s in Implementation and Outcome, to a 2 in Approach, and 3s in Implementation and Outcome in Information and Analysis.

Between the baseline assessment and the fall assessment, River Road administered questionnaires to all students, teachers, and parents. In the fall, the new technology coordinator attended hands-on data analysis workshops with the district data coordinator to learn how to analyze and chart questionnaire data. Besides analyzing and charting the questionnaire results, the technology coordinator and an interested teacher also charted student achievement results for the school.

Next Steps: Fall, Year Two

- We need to continue to administer and analyze questionnaire data for students, teachers, and parents to understand our client needs, to compile resulting charts in an interpreted organized way in our school portfolio, and to understand areas for improvement.

NOTES

It is useful to have the Continuous Improvement Continuums enlarged to poster size and affixed to the walls during the assessments. Staff members can then place colorful tags on the posters which show collectively where they believe the school is on each of the continuums. It is informative to see the diversity of thinking.

YEAR TWO

SCHOOL **portfolio** RTFOLIO

Being able to see progress keeps staff moving ahead and motivates them to make more progress.

Education for the Future provides hands-on and overview data analysis workshops to build the capacity of schools to do this work.

- We need to look at all K-5 data to get to the root causes of problems and to understand what we need to do to improve.
- We need to continue to build the capacity of several individuals in the school to do the data analysis work. There is too much work for one or two persons to do by themselves.

By spring, year two, staff felt that the school was a 3 in Approach, 3 in Implementation, and 3 in Outcome with respect to Information and Analysis. Historical standardized test scores and more Reading Recovery data have been added to the school database that was created this year. Staff are seeing the benefits of using these data. They, therefore, have committed personnel time out of their budget to continue developing the student achievement database to include authentic assessment and schoolwide Reading Recovery results, accessible to teachers at the classroom levels.

Next Steps: Spring, Year Two

- We need our school database to continue to give us historical disaggregated student achievement results for the school. Additionally this database has to allow us to follow the individual achievement scores of students, over time, including authentic assessment results for all teachers to use to study the impact of their school processes on students.
- We need to conduct a follow-up of our students after they leave River Road and make sure they are prepared for the next grade levels.
- We need to continue to build the capacity of many individuals in the school to do the data analysis work. There is too much work for one or two persons to do by themselves.
- We need to check with the district with respect to their interest in supporting a database person at the district level to benefit all schools.

SCHOOL **portfolio** RTFOLIO

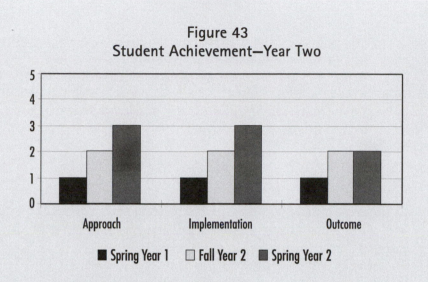

Figure 43
Student Achievement—Year Two

■ Spring Year 1   □ Fall Year 2   ■ Spring Year 2

NOTES

The time required to do these assessments decreases significantly as staff continue to assess their school on these continuums and work together on next steps. One school begins to emerge with common thinking.

Student Achievement

By the fall of year two, River Road staff rated the school a 2 in Approach with respect to Student Achievement, 2 in Implementation, and 2 in Outcome, largely because student learning standards were to be identified districtwide during the year. Staff feel that, overall, the instructional and assessment processes critical to student success still have not been identified for all content areas. Content standards are being identified, and performance standards will follow. Some student achievement gains are being noted. Learning gaps have been identified and instruction has been improved in program areas such as Reading Recovery.

Next Steps: Fall, Year Two

- We are on our way to identifying student learning standards, and in clarifying how to implement the vision at the school level. We cannot move ahead without the standards.
- We still need to increase communication across and within grade levels for a continuum of learning that makes sense for students.

NOTES

There is a point in time when the school will have difficulty making progress on the Continuous Improvement Continuums if they have not done the hard work of developing a shared vision and gathering and analyzing data about their processes.

By the spring of year two, the district had identified student learning and performance standards for language arts, and standards for math. A six-level rubric for writing had been identified and many teachers began to use portfolios with their students. Ideas on how to improve learning were identified and implemented. The results showed some student achievement gains. Staff felt that they had moved to a 3 in Approach, 3 in Implementation, but remained a 2 in Outcome.

Next Steps: Spring, Year Two

- We must learn to use the student achievement database that will allow us to follow the individual achievement scores of all students, over time.
- We need to enter authentic assessment scores into the database and track historical achievement of individual students.

SCHOOL **portfolio** RTFOLIO

A shared vision is one that means the same thing to everyone on staff. If the meaning has not been discussed and agreed upon, there is more than one vision being implemented.

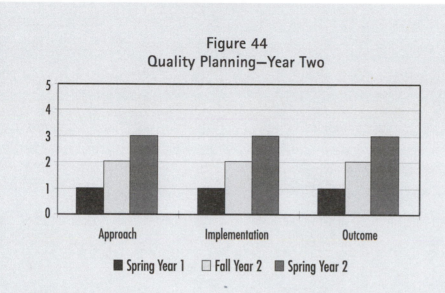

Figure 44
Quality Planning—Year Two

■ Spring Year 1   □ Fall Year 2   ■ Spring Year 2

Quality Planning

River Road staff rated the school 2s in Approach, Implementation, and Outcome in Quality Planning in the fall of year two. Staff were able to clarify a mission, vision, values, and beliefs during the summer and at an early fall retreat. During this year, a comprehensive action plan will be created.

Next Steps: Fall, Year Two

- We need to develop one comprehensive schoolwide plan.
- Staff need to make sure the vision, mission, and plan are in alignment.
- We will include teachers, administrators, parents, and students in the planning process and make sure everyone owns it.

SCHOOL **portfolio** RTFOLIO

Most schools agree that quality planning is one area where a small amount of work leads to the greatest payoffs. Plans make things happen.

By the spring of year two, staff felt that they had moved to 3s in Approach, Implementation, and Outcome in Quality Planning. During the year, a comprehensive school plan was developed to achieve the vision—complete with goals, responsibilities, due dates, and timelines. By the end of the year, there was already evidence that the school plan was being implemented in some areas and making a difference.

Next Steps: Spring, Year Two

- Now that we have a plan and vision, we must implement the vision throughout the school.

SCHOOL portfolio RTFOLIO

NOTES

Professional development tends to be one of the hardest habits to change in schools. Teachers like to hang onto the custom of attending conferences of their choice. Professional development focused on implementing the vision, is far more than conferences and workshops. Often, the most meaningful professional development occurs when teachers collaborate to change practice.

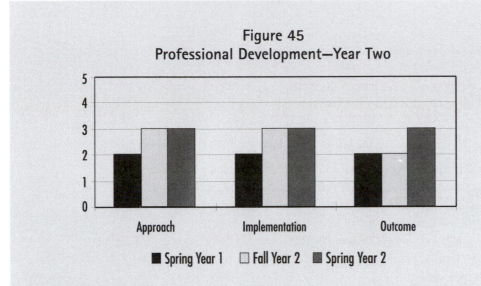

Figure 45
Professional Development—Year Two

■ Spring Year 1   □ Fall Year 2   ■ Spring Year 2

Professional Development

In fall, year two, staff felt that River Road school was a 3 in Approach and Implementation and 2 in Outcome in Professional Development, even with the schoolwide plan not being fully defined. Staff felt they have a new way of thinking about professional development and have already had some training in the summer and early fall in shared decision-making. With reading being a high priority for staff, we know we have to get more primary classroom teachers into Reading Recovery training so they can use the strategies with all students who can profit from the strategies. Our technology coordinator has been very helpful in training us in specific software packages. We all appreciate the fact that he is willing to coach us individually in our own classrooms. When the school plan is developed, it will include a long-range plan for professional development to help everyone understand what he or she needs to do to implement the vision.

Next Steps: Fall, Year Two

- Continue to build the school plan, from which the professional development plan will emerge.

YEAR TWO

SCHOOL portfolio RTFOLIO

By the spring of year two, with the school plan identified, a plan for professional development emerged. Because all the data necessary to inform the school goals were not entirely available, staff felt that they were still at the 3 level in Approach and Implementation, although more solid than in the fall, and had moved to a 3 in Outcome.

Next Steps: Spring, Year Two

- When the student achievement database is available to classroom teachers, it will be easier to identify what the students need and, in turn, what teachers need to better meet the needs of students.
- The professional development that we have to commit to has to be staffwide, related to the vision, and ongoing throughout the year.
- We must implement peer coaching along with the professional development training related to our vision in order to implement the vision of the school in a supportive fashion.

SCHOOL portfolio PORTFOLIO

NOTES

Time has to be allocated for the implementation of a vision and for shared decision-making. Banking time and having an "early out" day helps to make the time during the week.

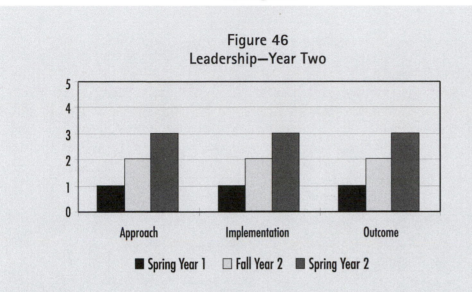

Figure 46
Leadership—Year Two

■ Spring Year 1   □ Fall Year 2   ■ Spring Year 2

Leadership

In the fall of year two staff felt that River Road was a 2 in Approach, a 2 in Implementation, and a 2 in Outcome, with respect to school Leadership. Staff were able to establish a leadership team committed to continuous improvement and one that seeks input from all school staff. Values and beliefs, and the mission and vision were identified by early fall, and student learning and performance standards will be identified during the school year. Teachers are becoming committed to continuous improvement.

Next Steps: Fall, Year Two

- A shared decision-making leadership structure needs to emerge that is in alignment with our values and beliefs, purpose, vision, mission, and plan.
- We need to study approaches to implementing the vision.

SCHOOL portfolio RTFOLIO

Designing a leadership structure that looks like the vision ensures the implementation of that vision. A vision will never be implemented if the leadership structure is incongruent with the vision.

By spring of year two, staff felt that Leadership was a 3 in Approach, 3 in Implementation, and a 3 in Outcome. During the year, the school plan was created and a leadership structure was built in alignment with it and the vision. All faculty were feeling included in decision-making by the end of the year. Study teams and a strong communication structure for keeping everyone informed were established. A plan for implementation is in place and critical areas for improvement have been identified for implementation in year three. Everyone on staff feels involved in and responsible for improving River Road school.

Next Steps: Spring, Year Two

- We need to make sure that year three starts with our identified leadership structure intact to set the tone for the whole year and to ensure the sustainability of the plans and structures.
- We need to make sure everyone understands his or her role in implementing the vision.

SCHOOL **portfolio** PORTFOLIO

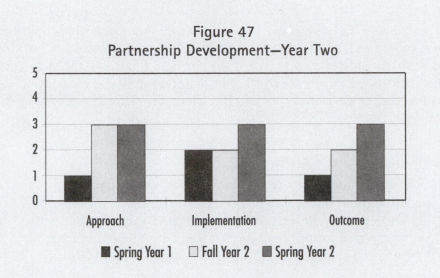

Figure 47
Partnership Development—Year Two

■ Spring Year 1   □ Fall Year 2   ■ Spring Year 2

Partnership Development

Partnership Development for the year two fall assessment placed Partnership Development at 3 in Approach, 2 in Implementation, and 2 in Outcome. A team has been assigned to get partners, schoolwide. The school knows why partnerships are important and seeks to include businesses and parents in a strategic fashion related to our vision. Our questionnaires are getting parent and community input into the school processes. Some things are happening with respect to partnerships, such as donated computer equipment.

Next Steps: Fall, Year Two

- We need to implement the partnership team's plan for partnerships.
- Our partnership development plan needs to be a part of the overall schoolwide plan that will assist us in achieving our student standards and in implementing our vision.

YEAR TWO

SCHOOL **portfolio** PORTFOLIO

Always remember to thank your partners. A simple thank you note is great!

By the spring of year two, the schoolwide plan, including partnership development had been created. Staff agreed on what they expect students to know and be able to do and a plan for partners related to the vision evolved almost effortlessly, ready for true implementation in year three. Staff knew that they had moved to 3s in Approach, Implementation, and Outcome by the end of the year.

Next Steps: Spring, Year Two

- We need to utilize parents, community, and businesses throughout our school in a systematic fashion.
- We need to make sure that all our partnerships are win-wins.
- We need to measure our partnership development to know if our partnerships are leading to increased student learning.

CONTINUOUS IMPROVEMENT

SCHOOL **portfolio** PORTFOLIO

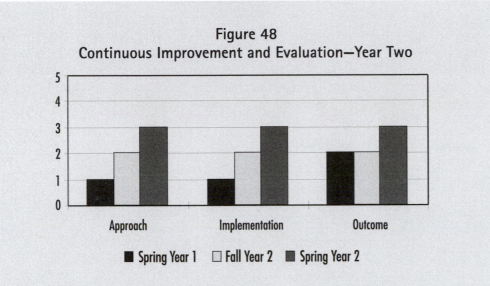

Figure 48
Continuous Improvement and Evaluation—Year Two

■ Spring Year 1   □ Fall Year 2   ■ Spring Year 2

Continuous Improvement and Evaluation

In the fall of year two, staff rated the school all 2s in Approach, Implementation, and Outcome in Continuous Improvement and Evaluation. Neither goals nor strategies currently exist for the evaluation and continuous improvement of the school, although this year's staff conversations and training will be about clarifying this. Staff are committed to continuous improvement and evaluation, but feel that most problems are still being solved with temporary solutions.

Next Steps: Fall, Year Two

- During this year, we will create our comprehensive database that will allow us to evaluate all aspects of our organization.
- We need to identify root causes of problems and understand what we need to do to get student achievement increases.

SCHOOL **portfolio** PORTFOLIO

NOTES

We measure what we treasure.

During the school year, the database and a comprehensive continuous improvement plan were created moving River Road to all 3s in Continuous Improvement and Evaluation. Some parts of the school have been evaluated for effectiveness and improved on the basis of evaluation results. Effective improvement strategies and results are obvious to staff.

Next Steps: Spring, Year Two

- We need to identify root causes of problems.
- We must implement our continuous improvement plan and evaluate all elements of the school organization for effectiveness and alignment.
- Continuous improvement data have to get to the classroom level so teachers can become astute at assessing and predicting the impact of their actions on students.

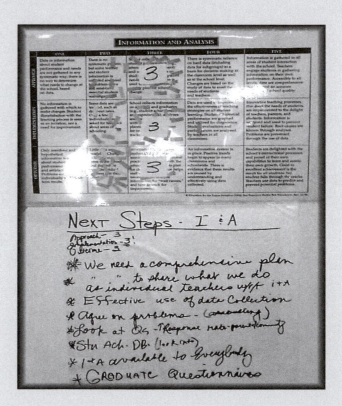

SCHOOL **portfolio** RTFOLIO

Summary and Next Steps
Continuous Improvement Continuum Assessment Year Two

Members of the River Road School staff conducted their assessments on the Education for the Future Initiative Continuous Improvement Continuums twice during the second continuous improvement school year. As with the baseline assessment, each staff person made her/his personal rating about the school. Staff members discussed why they thought the school was where they rated it. The staff came to consensus on a number that represented where the entire school was, for each of the sections. A summary of the results follows.

Overall Next Steps:

- We need to input individual student achievement data in the school database and utilize the analyses at the classroom level.
- We need to enter all measures of student learning into our school database.
- We need to focus on implementing our schoolwide vision and plan.
- We need to update our school leadership structure.
- We need to make sure our partners are getting what they need out of the partnership.
- We need to implement our comprehensive improvement and analysis system.

YEAR THREE

SCHOOL portfolio PORTFOLIO

River Road Elementary School
Continuous Improvement Continuums Assessment
Year Three

Members of the River Road staff conducted their assessments of the school on the Education for the Future Initiative Continuous Improvement Continuums twice during their third continuous improvement school year. As with the previous two years, each staff person made her/his personal rating, then staff members discussed why they thought the school was where they rated it. The staff came to consensus on a number that represented where the entire school is on each of the sections. The ratings and brief discussions for each Education for the Future Continuous Improvement Continuum follow.

SCHOOL **portfolio** RTFOLIO

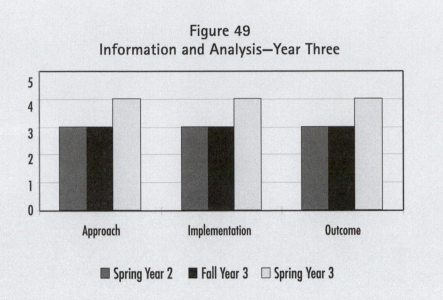

Figure 49
Information and Analysis—Year Three

■ Spring Year 2   ■ Fall Year 3   ☐ Spring Year 3

Information and Analysis

Collectively, staff felt that starting year three, River Road merited 3s in Approach, Implementation, and Outcome with respect to Information and Analysis. Historical data have been charted to show the performance of individual students and cohorts of students, over time. These data are used for early identification of students who are having difficulties learning so that interventions can be made to prevent their failure later on. This discussion has led to the continuum of learning all teachers want for the children.

Next Steps: Fall, Year Three

- We need to collect multiple measures of data from all teachers systematically on a schoolwide basis, and look at all K-5 data to ensure the sustainability of the continuum of learning we need and want for all students.
- We need to continue building our database so that it is easy for teachers to access for their own students, and so they can look, over time, to understand the big picture when desired.

SCHOOL portfolio RTFOLIO

Without data, the same processes are used, with the expectation that different results will occur, or random acts of improvement are attempted and may or may not result in improved outcomes.

By spring of year three, an excellent student achievement database was in place and accessible to all teachers. Authentic assessment results have been included in the database. Root causes of problems are able to be identified. With the database, some teachers have begun to engage in teacher action research, are learning to assess the impact of their actions on students, and know what they need to do to get different results. Special programs and interventions are now able to be evaluated. Staff was unanimous in believing that River Road had reached solid 4s in Approach, Implementation, and Outcome by the spring of year three.

Next Steps: Spring, Year Three

- We must never allow our school to go back to not using data. We have made constant student achievement gains with most groups, and where there was a problem, we have been able to identify the specific issues that we had to address, .

SCHOOL **portfolio** RTFOLIO

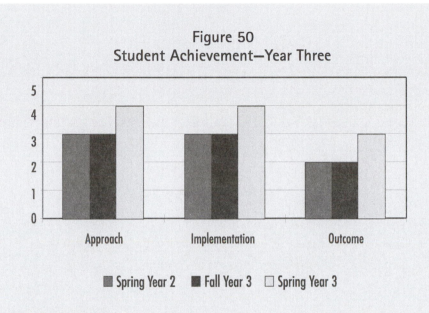

Figure 50
Student Achievement—Year Three

Student Achievement

By the fall of year three, staff was using student achievement data throughout the school to understand how to improve student learning. Teachers were collaborating to implement appropriate instruction and assessment strategies for meeting the student learning standards. Some teachers plan to begin teaming together for peer coaching. Through all aspects of the school, there is a positive focus on the improvement of student learning. Student achievement and satisfaction with the learning environment are increasing. Because of these facts, staff felt that River Road maintained their rating of 3 on the continuum, but felt they would be rated higher on this continuum by spring, year three.

Next Steps: Fall, Year Three

- We need to make sure the use of data and the implementation of the vision's instructional and assessment strategies are systemic and in every classroom.
- We must encourage peer coaching and action research throughout the school.

YEAR THREE

SCHOOL portfolio RTFOLIO

NOTES

Agreeing on what we expect our students to know and be able to do, and how we will know that they can do it, clarifies how the staff will support students in their learning.

By spring, year three, all teachers had been peer coached at least once. There is evidence systemwide that effective instructional and assessment strategies are being implemented in most classrooms. The standards and assessments are also helping. Many peer coaching teams were in existence.

Everywhere, teachers are talking about preventing student failure and what they are learning about getting student achievement increases. Staff rated the school as solid 4s in Approach and Implementation, and a 3 in Outcome.

Next Steps: Spring, Year Three

- Teachers need to move to formalize their action research.
- Teachers need to conduct comparative analyses of actual student performance to the district standards.

CONTINUOUS IMPROVEMENT

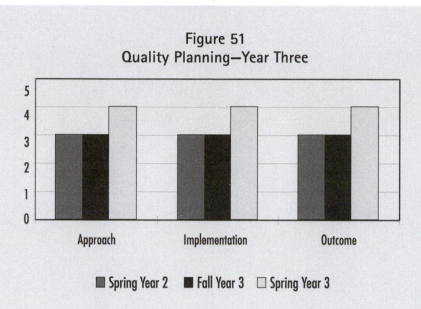

NOTES

When a vision is clear and shared, and the action it takes to implement the vision is determined, the vision gets implemented much faster than anticipated.

Figure 51
Quality Planning—Year Three

■ Spring Year 2   ■ Fall Year 3   □ Spring Year 3

Quality Planning

In the fall of year three, staff felt that their schoolwide plan was solid and ready for implementation schoolwide. Everyone was clear on the school goals and their role in implementing them. Staff felt that they were solid 3s in Approach, Implementation, and Outcome.

Next Steps: Fall, Year Three

- We need to support everyone's implementation of the school plan, and make sure everyone understands the plan in the same way.
- We need to follow through on timelines, due dates, and responsibilities.

By spring of year three, every teacher was implementing elements of the vision. The results of working toward the quality improvement goals were evident. Staff felt they were solid 4s on this continuum by spring of year three.

Next Steps: Spring, Year Three

- We need to reinforce the articulation of all aspects of the school.
- We need to follow our students to the next levels and learn how we can continuously improve what we do.

YEAR THREE

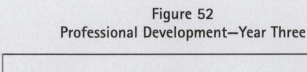

When a school creates a shared vision, a staff developer/facilitator can work onsite with all staff toward implementing their vision. This outside facilitator's role is to help everyone in the organization understand her/his role in implementing the vision, and to help staff reflect on their current practices using data to identify the gaps between what they want to be doing and what they are doing. This is the only way to ensure the true and thorough implementation of a vision.

Figure 52
Professional Development—Year Three

■ Spring Year 2　■ Fall Year 3　☐ Spring Year 3

Professional Development

In the fall of year three, River Road staff assessed the school on Professional Development as a 3 in Approach, 3 in Implementation, and 3 in Outcome.

During the summer and in early fall, new directions in professional development started to be implemented. A trainer was brought in to provide professional development to all staff members with respect to our vision . This training incorporated the data we have been gathering and allowed staff to talk about student achievement data, the vision, and our standards. During teacher team time, staff set goals for implementing ways to support each other and established schedules for peer coaching each other in the new strategies. A collegial school, focused on student learning, was becoming quite evident.

Next steps: Fall, Year Three

- We need to continue to engage in professional development related to our vision and overall school plan; to coach each other in the implementation of instruction and assessment strategies; and to perfect the way we gather and use data to research approaches to increasing student achievement.
- We would like to begin action research to support the ongoing measuring of how we are doing for students.

SCHOOL portfolio PORTFOLIO

Action research is an exciting way for teachers to use data to improve what they do to increase student learning.

During year three, a core of teachers was able to implement action research as they utilized data and implemented new instructional and assessment strategies. This was sooner than they thought they would be able to do this. However, because their plan for the implementation of the vision was so strong, they were also able to begin to utilize the action research/peer coaching combination to replace their traditional approach to teacher evaluation. River Road teachers are now passionate about what they can do to make sure they are reaching every student in the best way possible. Staff unanimously voted that River Road is now 4s in Approach, Implementation, and Outcome in Professional Development.

Next Steps: Spring, Year Three

We know the power of this work. Because of the impact on student achievement, we can never go back to the old ways of doing business. We also know that if our leaders or staff change, this is still the way we do business at River Road. This portfolio documents our approach that will assist any new staff member in implementing what the veteran staff is doing. These changes are definitely systemic.
- Continue to do the work.
- Continue to evaluate the effectiveness of our professional development with respect to implementing the vision.

SCHOOL **portfolio** PORTFOLIO

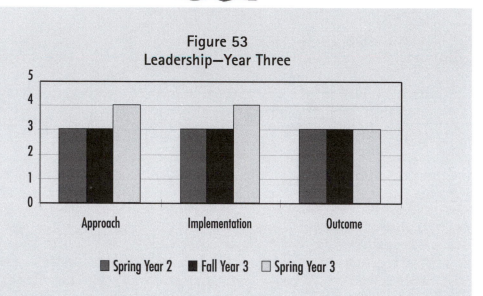

Figure 53
Leadership—Year Three

■ Spring Year 2   ■ Fall Year 3   □ Spring Year 3

Leadership

In fall of year three, staff felt that River Road was a 3 in Approach, 3 in Implementation, and 3 in Outcome, with respect to school Leadership. River Road's leadership structure appeared to be working, but had not been tried enough to warrant 4s at the beginning of the year.

Next Steps: Fall, Year Three

- We need to clarify and implement our leadership structure for the school that respects and is acceptable to all individuals in the school.
- We need to clarify roles and responsibilities of all members of the school.

In the spring of year three, staff felt that the school had moved to 4s in Approach and Implementation, but not quite a 4 in Outcome. The true shared decision-making structure needs another year to really know if it is systemic or not. Also, our student learning standards have not all been identified yet.

SCHOOL portfolio RTFOLIO

Next Steps: Spring, Year Three

- We need to continue to implement our leadership structure and to focus on its linkages to student standards and the guiding principles of the school.
- We need to evaluate the effectiveness of our shared decision-making structure and to involve more of the school community and district office in our decisions.

NOTES

It is the leader's job to make sure everyone in the organization understands that it is her/his job to implement the vision.

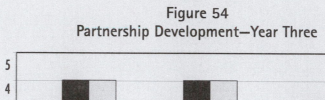

Figure 54
Partnership Development—Year Three

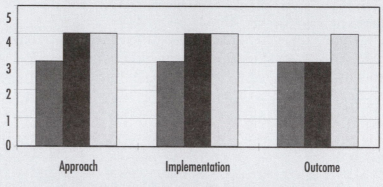

Partnership Development

Staff rated the school 4s in Approach and Implementation, and a 3 in Outcome with respect to Partnership Development in the fall of year three. Staff agreed that the school's efforts in seeking effective community/business partnerships and effective parent involvement have been beneficial to both parties. All staff are clear on what is desired with respect to parent involvement and business/community outcomes. Some student achievement increases can be attributed to partnerships.

Next Steps: Fall, Year Three

- We must implement a systematic and systemic way to measure the impact of River Road's partnerships on student achievement.

In the spring of year three, staff felt that the school was solid 4s in Approach, Implementation, and Outcome.

Next Steps: Spring, Year Three

- We must make sure that we are connecting to all the partners that make sense for our students' learning.

SCHOOL **portfolio** PORTFOLIO

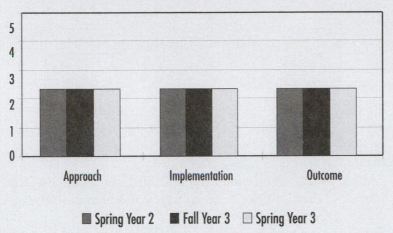

Figure 55
Continuous Improvement and Evaluation—Year Three

■ Spring Year 2   ■ Fall Year 3   ☐ Spring Year 3

NOTES

There is nothing more disappointing than to get evaluation results at the end of the year that point to things that could have been improved during the year. Continuous improvement and evaluation helps everyone know what to do to improve on an ongoing basis.

Continuous Improvement and Evaluation

In fall, year three, staff was proud that they were evaluating elements of the school and improving the elements on the basis of their evaluation. With the database intact, staff could analyze the root causes of problems and improve program elements. Positive changes were being made and it felt like the results could be maintained. Staff agreed to 3s across the board for Approach, Implementation, and Outcome in Continuous Improvement and Evaluation.

Next Steps: Fall, Year Three

- We need to evaluate all elements of the school for improvement and ensure congruence of the elements with respect to our vision and student learning standards.
- We need to continue to develop a continuum of learning that makes sense for students.

YEAR THREE

SCHOOL **portfolio** RTFOLIO

All parts of the learning organization must be connected. If one part is out of alignment with the vision, the vision may never be accomplished. Assessing on the Continuous Improvement Continuums will help you know if all parts are in alignment.

In spring of year three, staff had experienced almost an entire year of using data to improve instruction. Although improvements were noted everywhere, we were not sure if the positive changes would be sustainable at all grade levels. Because of that, we chose to rate the school as 4s and not 5s in Approach, Implementation, and Outcome for Continuous Improvement and Evaluation.

Next Steps: Spring, Year Three

- We must continue our work with data and evaluating every aspect of the school. We must continually train and retrain ourselves to assess uniformly on our student rubrics so that the assessment data is meaningful.
- Teachers must become astute at assessing and predicting the impact of their instructional strategies on individual student achievement.
- We need to continue to work toward becoming a congruent and effective learning organization.

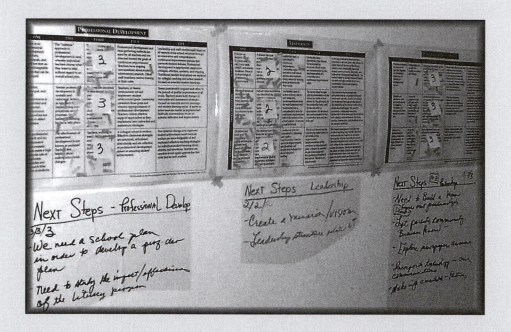

SCHOOL **portfolio** PORTFOLIO

Summary and Next Steps
Continuous Improvement Continuum Assessment
Year Three

Members of the River Road School staff conducted their assessments of where the school is on the Education for the Future Initiative Continuous Improvement Continuums twice during the third continuous improvement school year. As with the previous years' assessments, each staff person made her/his personal rating about the school. Staff members discussed why they thought the school was where they rated it. The staff came to consensus on a number that represented where the entire school was, for each of the sections. A summary of the results follows.

Overall Next Steps: Year Three

- We need to continue inputting all measures of individual student learning data in the school database and utilizing the analyses at the classroom level.
- We need to continue to support teacher action research and peer coaching in order to implement the vision in an articulated fashion.
- We need to continue to measure actual student performance against the district and school standards.
- We need to follow our students into the middle school, high school, and beyond to ensure that their early education was as beneficial to them as it could be.
- We must continue to support and implement the schoolwide plan, vision, shared decision-making, and a continuum of learning that makes sense for all students.
- We must never lose sight of our guiding principles. Our continuous improvement and evaluation process will help us make sure we stay on target.

The School Portfolio and the Continuous Improvement Continuums are continuous improvement tools that help everyone know where the school is, where it is going, and what it is doing to get there.

Continuous Improvement and Evaluation Summary from the Authors' Perspectives

River Road Progress

Twice each year River Road staff assessed where they were on the Education for the Future Initiative Continuous Improvement Continuums. After each assessment, next steps were determined and documented. The clarity of the desired next steps led to the implementation of the next steps—almost immediately. Consequently, the subsequent assessment showed improvement.

One of the greatest benefits to River Road staff in conducting assessments on the Continuous Improvement Continuums was that staff could see how the parts of the learning organization work together. They could see that one piece not in place could keep progress from being made in all other areas. For example, until River Road clarified a vision there could be no schoolwide plan or appropriate professional development determined; without a plan and appropriate professional development there could be no systematic implementation of new approaches in the classroom. Staff realized also that until a vision is shared, there is no one vision.

This staff additionally discovered that, without data, any adjustments made to processes are just best guesses. The use of data was a real eye-opener for staff. The data showed teachers what changes to make to get different results. The data gave them reasons to celebrate their successes.

River Road staff like assessing with the Continuous Improvement Continuums because it gives them a gauge of where they were when they started, where they are right now, and where they are going. They celebrate progress while planning for more implementation. The more progress they make, the more they want to make.

Another reason River Road staff like using the Continuous Improvement Continuums is the fact that the continuums help their concrete-sequential learners see steps along a continuum; it helps ground their next steps without being tied to a step-by-step process. Just looking at goals or the vision is too global for some teachers.

Items for the Continuous Improvement and Evaluation Section

The Continuous Improvement and Evaluation section of your school portfolio is where staff assess where the school is as a learning organization. It is a section that allows you to sit back and look at the big picture, what needs to happen next, and what is causing parts to not work together. Items that might go in this section include the following:

- Assessments on the Education for the Future Continuous Improvement Continuums and discussion about priorities and next steps
- Analyses of progress
- Evaluation results of programs or processes
- Plans for continuous improvement
- Systems thinking analyses
- Accomplishments for the year
- Goals for improvement/next steps

Making the Difference for Continuous Improvement

Documenting next steps is infectious. So is making progress. The Continuous Improvement Continuums help with both. By clarifying the goal for each section (i.e., the 5 in Outcome), staff can understand and share that goal, measure where they are right now with respect to that goal, and then determine what they need to do to move closer to the goal. As long as staff are clear about where they are going, and the measurement tool represents that goal, the tool is a wonderful vehicle for helping them get there. A safe and confidential environment must be established to reap the greatest benefits.

Recommendations

In putting together a school portfolio, we recommend that schools assess where they are on the Continuous Improvement Continuums (or some other measurement tool) for many reasons.

- This measurement tool gives staff a clear and shared idea of where they are going. One of the reasons continuous improvement efforts fail is that a shared vision and common goals are missing. The continuums offer goals and a means to discuss what it will look like when the goals are implemented, and the benefits and identifiable points along the way.
- The discussion around the continuums clarifies what to document in each section of the school portfolio—a rating results as well as what needs to be documented in each section.
- All staff can participate and hear at the same time how the parts work together to create a whole.
- As staff consider why they rate the school a specific number, other staff hear their perspective. They are able to discuss what needs to happen to move the entire school in the same direction.
- The continuums give the staff a chance to see that they are making progress. Too many staffs give up on continuous improvement because they are unable to see that they are making progress.
- The continuums help staff see how much farther they have to go to get to their goals.
- Whenever staff lay out next steps, the next steps are completed.

Part 3
Summary
and Conclusions

Chapter 11
Summary

Summary
from the Authors' Perspectives

What you have witnessed in this book is one (fictitious) elementary school working toward school improvement using a school portfolio that documents their progress in becoming a continuously improving school. While the authors showed how this process works with an elementary school, it can be used with any school or district, and at any grade level. The school portfolio works equally well in urban, suburban, low income, wealthy, small, and large schools and districts. It also works with programs and projects, although we prefer to take a comprehensive look at the entire learning organization.

This chapter takes the process full circle by describing:
- River Road progress
- A review of the school portfolio
- The mechanics of building a school portfolio
- Recommendations
- Conclusions

River Road Progress

River Road Elementary School started without real support from their leadership and without the data support they so dearly needed. They evolved over three years into a school that is ready for truly significant changes to be taking place in the core of their learning organization. They saw only slight student achievement gains, but are prime to see many more in the future.

Without school and district leadership support, River Road did not make quantum leaps of progress. They could have, had they collected their data together earlier, and had they come to consensus on their guiding principles and plan during the first year.

This staff would have benefited greatly from an overview of the school portfolio as they started. They would have known how to look for the connections of school elements, and they would have known they needed to gather historical student achievement data for their efforts. Even without clear guidance, River Road staff persisted and soon understood that major elements of change come from within by changing how the organization actually works. They learned together to think differently about their students, to collaborate, to use data to solve problems, and to plan and implement change in their teaching practices.

Review of the School Portfolio

The discussion below is a review of the elements in a school portfolio and why they are important.

Information and Analysis is a critical element in planning for change and in supporting continual school improvement. This section builds the context of the school, clarifies who they are as a school community, who the students are and the results of current processes. Schools need to start with the data they already have— basic demographics, historical achievement, and enrollment trends. Questionnaires that assess current and desired practices can be administered to students, teachers, and parents and charted responses placed in this section. It is crucial that as a learning organization begins this journey they understand who their clients are, and commit to meeting their needs. A school cannot be a service to the community and to the children it strives to serve if the teachers do not know who the students are. Information and analysis needs powerful statements of who the students are. The portfolio does not have teeth without these data or data about student achievement results.

Student Achievement describes the processes for increasing student learning. In this section, schools demonstrate how they are serving their students, and the why behind the chosen curriculum and instructional strategies. This is also where the vision is clarified as is how the learning organization plans to implement the vision.

Quality Planning describes the school's guiding principles; values and beliefs and purpose; a mission that describes the purpose of the school; a vision; goals that promote the mission and vision; and, an action plan needed to implement the vision. Learning organizations have one vision, everything in the organization needs to be targeted to that vision, including the budget.

Professional Development helps staff members, teachers, and principals change the manner in which they work; how they make decisions; how they gather, analyze, and utilize data; how they plan, teach, and monitor achievement; and how they evaluate personnel and assess the impact of new approaches to instruction and student assessment. Professional development is the key to implementing the vision.

Leadership focuses on creating a learning environment that encourages everyone to contribute to schools having a cumulative, purposeful effect on student learning. With strong leaders, learning organizations can create new beginnings to get outstanding results. Educational leaders—principals, superintendents, teachers— need to think in terms of how do we want to leave this world 200 years from now.

They have to be advocates for the children; guardians of children who do not have families; and guardians of the children who have families who do not know how to support their childrens' learning. Leadership needs to keep the focus on things that matter.

Partnership Development describes the school's purpose for, approach to, and plans for educational partnerships with businesses, the community, parents, students, and other educational professionals. It is important to plan for partnerships and to seek to get involved with partners to implement the vision.

Continuous Improvement and Evaluation is the section that pulls all the pieces together. Continuous improvement and evaluation analyzes the entire school as a learning organization, assesses plans, implementation, processes, and progress to determine what needs to improve and how to make those improvements. It also indicates how all the parts of the organization work together for students.

Assessing on the Continuous Improvement Continuums is an easy way to get an objective idea of where the school is, to determine what the school has with respect to each category and other evidence they want to collect, to determine where they want to go from where they are, to understand how the parts are working together and how they can get the parts to work together.

Mechanics of Putting a School Portfolio Together

Before beginning the process of creating a school portfolio, think about how you want it to go together. Focusing the portfolio around measurement continuums is a nice approach. River Road staff set up their school portfolio to add on to each year, with the exception of one section, Information and Analysis. This section gives a little history of their work with data that remains in their school portfolio. The charts are updated each year to capture recent history.

In the *The School Portfolio: A Comprehensive Framework for School Improvement* (Second Edition) Chapter 11 is devoted to the details of putting together and maintaining a school portfolio. Additionally, Appendix B provides many helpful suggestions about the mechanics and formatting of your portfolio.

Recommendations

In an ideal situation, leadership would be working with staff to continuously improve and would link up with an outside organization to assist with their school improvement efforts. Working with an outside organization gives the school improvement effort a flavor of intrigue, excitement, and urgency to change. It also seals the commitment to make the change. A school coach, possibly from the district office, can also greatly assist with the school improvement process. The coach or outside organization could help with data and objectively ensure that the process and the work make sense.

As an overview of the process is relayed, staff can determine what they have and what information they need to gather for the parts of the process. It is crucial to have leadership buy-in. With leadership buy-in, old agendas and assumptions can be laid to rest and the data can be obtained that are needed for your continuous improvement journey.

In the ideal situation, staff would begin by being clear on who their students are. This could be done by conducting research or reading about different cultures, analyzing questionnaire results, being set up to conduct data analyses to understand student achievement results, and beginning to map their processes against these results.

Conclusion

The school portfolio is an effective way to tell the story of the school (or district) and to document the progress, processes, and products of the school. One of the beauties of the school portfolio is that any school can start where they are and build from there. The documentation of where they are in each section and where they want to be helps everyone see the same school. It also assists with the alignment of all the pieces.

The portfolio helps with the communication process for everyone in the learning organization, for the community, district, state, accreditation agencies, funders.

The School Portfolio keeps the momentum of school improvement flowing.

Appendix A
Continuous
Improvement
Continuums

Continuous Improvement Continuums

These Education for the Future Initiative Continuous Improvement Continuums[4], adapted from the Malcolm Baldrige Award Program for Quality Business Management, provide an authentic means for measuring schoolwide improvement and growth. In conjunction with a school portfolio, schools use these continuums as a vehicle for ongoing self-assessment. They use the results of the assessment to acknowledge their accomplishments, to set goals for improvement, and to keep school districts and partners apprised of the progress they have made in their school improvement efforts.

The Education for the Future Initiative Continuous Improvement Continuums (CICs) are a type of rubric that represents the theoretical flow of systemic school improvement. The continuums (see Tables A1 through A7 on the pages following) are made up of seven key, interrelated, and overlapping components of systemic change—Information and Analysis, Student Achievement, Quality Planning, Professional Development, Leadership, Partnership Development, and Continuous Improvement and Evaluation.

Understanding the Continuums

These rubrics, extending from *one* to *five* horizontally, represent a continuum of expectations related to school improvement with respect to an *approach* to the continuum, *implementation* of the approach, and the *outcome* that results from the implementation. A *one* rating, located at the left of each continuum, represents a school that has not yet begun to improve. *Five*, located at the right of each continuum, represents a school that is one step removed from "world class quality." The elements between *one* and *five* describe how that continuum is hypothesized to evolve in a continuously improving school. Each continuum moves from a reactive mode to a proactive mode—from fire fighting to prevention. The five in outcome in each continuum is the target.

Vertically, the *approach, implementation,* and *outcome* statements, for any number *one* through *five*, are hypotheses. In other words, the *implementation* statement describes how the *approach* might look when implemented, and the *outcome* is the "pay-off" for implementing the approach. If the hypotheses are accurate, the outcome will not be realized until the approach is actually implemented.

---

[4]The Education for the Future Initiative Continuous Improvement Continuums and the School Portfolio are described in *The School Portfolio: A Comprehensive Framework for School Improvement*, Second Edition, published by Eye on Education, 6 Depot Way West, Suite 106, Larchmont, NY 10538. Tel. (914) 833-0551.

Using the Continuums

The most valuable way to use the continuums is to have all staff rate the school together. First have each member of the staff make their personal rating of where they feel the school as a whole is on each continuum. Take a quick count of how many feel this school is a *one* in *approach* to Information and Analysis, a *two*, and so on. If all staff agree on the same number, record the number and rationale, and move on. If there is a discrepancy, ask for discussion. The discussion clarifies what is happening schoolwide with respect to the continuum. The goal is to get a number that represents the rating that everyone can live with. The discussion and documentation of next steps are more important than the actual number that results. The ultimate goal is to make all aspects of the school consistent and congruent with the vision. Assessing your school on the Continuous Improvement Continuums at least twice each year is recommended.

Using these continuums will enable you and your school to stay motivated, to shape and maintain your shared vision, and assist with the continuous improvement of all elements of your school.

Remember that where your school is at any time is where it is. The important thing is what you do with this information. Continuous improvement is a never-ending process which, when used effectively and for the right purpose, will ultimately lead your school toward providing a quality program for all children.

Table A1
Information and Analysis

	ONE	TWO	THREE	FOUR	FIVE
APPROACH	Data or information about student performance and needs are not gathered in any systematic way; there is no way to determine what needs to change at the school, based on data.	There is no systematic process, but some teacher and student information is collected and used to problem-solve and establish student learning standards.	School collects data related to student performance (e.g., attendance, achievement) and conducts surveys on student, teacher, and parent needs. The information is used to drive the strategic quality plan for school change.	There is systematic reliance on hard data (including data for subgroups) as a basis for decision-making at the classroom level as well as at the school level. Changes are based on the study of data to meet the needs of students and teachers.	Information is gathered in all areas of student interaction with the school. Teachers engage students in gathering information on their own performance. Accessible to all levels, data are comprehensive in scope and an accurate reflection of school quality.
IMPLEMENTATION	No information is gathered with which to make changes. Student dissatisfaction with the learning process is seen as an irritation, not a need for improvement.	Some data are tracked, such as dropout rates and enrollment. Only a few individuals are asked for feedback about areas of schooling.	School collects information on current and former students (e.g., student achievement and perceptions), analyzes and uses it in conjunction with future trends for planning. Identified areas for improvement are tracked over time.	Data are used to improve the effectiveness of teaching strategies on all student learning. Students' historical performances are graphed and utilized for diagnostics. Student evaluations and performances are analyzed by teachers in all classrooms.	Innovative teaching processes that meet the needs of students are implemented to the delight of teachers, parents, and students. Information is analyzed and used to prevent student failure. Root causes are known through analyses. Problems are prevented through the use of data.
OUTCOME	Only anecdotal and hypothetical information is available about student performance, behavior, and satisfaction. Problems are solved individually with short-term results.	Little data are available. Change is limited to some areas of the school and dependent upon individual teachers and their efforts.	Information collected about student and parent needs, assessment, and instructional practices are shared with the school staff and used to plan for change. Information helps staff understand pressing issues, analyze information for "root causes," track results for improvement.	An information system is in place. Positive trends begin to appear in many classrooms and schoolwide. There is evidence that these results are caused by understanding and effectively using data collected.	Students are delighted with the school's instructional processes and proud of their own capabilities to learn and assess their own growth. Good to excellent achievement is the result for all students. No student falls through the cracks. Teachers use data to predict and prevent potential problems.

Education for the Future Initiative, Chico CA (1994). Rev. 3/99

Table A2
Student Achievement

	ONE	TWO	THREE	FOUR	FIVE
APPROACH	Instructional and organizational processes critical to student success are not identified. Little distinction of student learning differences is made. Some teachers believe that not all students can achieve.	Some data are collected on student background and performance trends. Learning gaps are noted to direct improvement of instruction. It is known that student learning standards must be identified.	Student learning standards are identified and a continuum of learning is created throughout the school. Student performance data are collected and compared to the standards in order to analyze how to improve learning for all students.	Data on student achievement are used throughout the school to pursue the improvement of student learning. Teachers collaborate to implement appropriate instruction and assessment strategies for meeting student learning standards articulated across grade levels. All teachers believe that all students can learn.	School makes an effort to exceed student achievement expectations. Innovative instructional changes are made to anticipate learning needs and improve student achievement. Teachers are able to predict characteristics impacting student achievement and to know how to perform from a small set of internal quality measures.
IMPLEMENTATION	All students are taught the same way. There is no communication with students about their academic needs or learning styles. There are no analyses of how to improve instruction.	Some effort is made to track and analyze student achievement trends on a schoolwide basis. Teachers begin to understand the needs and learning gaps of students.	Teachers study effective instruction and assessment strategies to increase their students' learning. Student feedback and analysis of achievement data are used in conjunction with implementation support strategies.	There is a systematic focus on the improvement of student learning schoolwide. Effective instruction and assessment strategies are implemented in each classroom. Teachers support one another with peer coaching and/or action research focused on implementing strategies that lead to increased achievement.	All teachers correlate critical instructional and assessment strategies with objective indicators of quality student achievement. A comparative analysis of actual individual student performance to student learning standards is utilized to adjust teaching strategies to ensure a progression of learning for all students.
OUTCOME	There is wide variation in student attitudes and achievement with undesirable results. There is high dissatisfaction among students with learning. Student background is used as an excuse for low student achievement.	There is some evidence that student achievement trends are available to teachers and are being used. There is much effort, but minimal observable results in improving student achievement.	There is an increase in communication between students and teachers regarding student learning. Teachers learn about effective instructional strategies that will meet the needs of their students. They make some gains.	Increased student achievement is evident schoolwide. Student morale, attendance, and behavior are good. Teachers converse often with each other about preventing student failure. Areas for further attention are clear.	Students and teachers conduct self-assessments to continuously improve performance. Improvements in student achievement are evident and clearly caused by teachers' and students' understandings of individual student learning, linked to appropriate and effective instructional and assessment strategies. A continuum of learning results. No students fall through the cracks.

Education for the Future Initiative, Chico CA (1994). Rev. 3/99

Table A3
Quality Planning

	ONE	TWO	THREE	FOUR	FIVE
APPROACH	No quality plan or process exists. Data are neither used nor considered important in planning.	The staff realizes the importance of a mission, vision, and one comprehensive action plan. Teams develop goals and timelines, and dollars are allocated to begin the process.	A comprehensive school plan to achieve the vision is developed. Plan includes evaluation and continuous improvement.	One focused and integrated schoolwide plan for implementing a continuous improvement process is put into action. All school efforts are focused on the implementation of this plan that represents the achievement of the vision.	A plan for the continuous improvement of the school, with a focus on students, is put into place. There is excellent articulation and integration of all elements in the school due to quality planning. Leadership team ensures all elements are implemented by all appropriate parties.
IMPLEMENTATION	There is no knowledge of or direction for quality planning. Budget is allocated on an as-needed basis. Many plans exist.	School community begins continuous improvement planning efforts by laying out major steps to a shared vision, by identifying values and beliefs, the purpose of the school, a mission, vision, and student learning standards.	Implementation goals, responsibilities, due dates, and timelines are spelled out. Support structures for implementing the plan are set in place.	The quality management plan is implemented through effective procedures in all areas of the school. Everyone knows what she/he needs to do, and when it needs to be done to accomplish the school goals.	Schoolwide goals, mission, vision, and student learning standards are shared and articulated throughout the school and with feeder schools. The attainment of identified student learning standards is linked to planning and implementation of effective instruction that meets students' needs.
OUTCOME	There is no evidence of comprehensive planning. Staff work is carried out in isolation. A continuum of learning for students is absent.	The school community understands the benefits of working together to implement a comprehensive continuous improvement plan.	There is evidence that the school plan is being implemented in some areas of the school. Improvements are neither systematic nor integrated schoolwide.	A schoolwide plan is known to all. Results from working toward the quality improve-ment goals are evident throughout the school.	Evidence of effective teaching and learning results in significant improvement of student achievement attributed to quality planning at all levels of the school organization. Teachers understand and share the school mission and vision, the impact and importance of quality planning, and accountability.

Education for the Future Initiative, Chico CA (1994). Rev. 3/99

Table A4
Professional Development

	ONE	TWO	THREE	FOUR	FIVE
APPROACH	There is no professional development. Teachers, principals, and staff are seen as interchangeable parts that can be replaced.	The "cafeteria" approach to professional development is used, whereby individual teachers choose what they want to take, without regard to an overall school plan.	The school plan and student needs are used to target appropriate professional development for all employees. Staff is inserviced in relevant instructional and leadership strategies.	Professional development and data-gathering methods are used by all teachers and are directed toward the goals of continuous improvement. Teachers have ongoing conversations about student achievement research. Other staff members receive training in their roles.	Leadership and staff continuously improve all aspects of the school structure through an innovative and comprehensive continuous improvement process that prevents student failures. Professional development is appropriate for implementing the vision, supportive, collegial, effective, systemic, and ongoing. Traditional teacher evaluations are replaced by collegial coaching and action research focused on student learning standards.
IMPLEMENTATION	Teacher, principal, and staff performance is controlled and inspected. Performance evaluations are used to detect mistakes.	Teacher professional development is sporadic and unfocused, lacking an approach for implementing new procedures and processes. Some leadership training begins to take place.	Teachers are involved in year-round quality professional development. The school community is trained in shared decision making, team building concepts, and effective communication strategies.	Teachers, in teams, continuously set and implement student achievement goals. Leadership considers these goals and ensures appropriateness of professional development. Teachers utilize effective support approaches as they implement new instruction and assessment strategies.	Teams passionately support each other in the pursuit of quality improvement at all levels. Teachers make bold changes in instruction and assessment strategies focused on student learning standards and student learning styles. A teacher as action researcher model is implemented. Staffwide conversations focus on systemic reflection and improvement.
OUTCOME	No professional growth and no performance improvement. There exists a high turnover rate of employees. Attitudes and approach filter down to students.	The effectiveness of professional development is not known or analyzed. Teachers feel helpless about making schoolwide changes.	Teachers, working in teams, feel supported and begin to feel they can make changes. Evidence shows that shared decision-making works.	A collegial school is evident. Effective classroom strategies are practiced, articulated schoolwide, and are reflective of professional development aimed at ensuring student achievement.	True systemic change and improved student achievement result because teachers are knowledgeable of and implement effective teaching strategies for individual student learning styles, abilities, and situations. Teachers are sensitive to and apply approaches that work best for each student.

Education for the Future Initiative, Chico CA (1994). Rev. 3/99

Table A5
Leadership

	ONE	TWO	THREE	FOUR	FIVE
APPROACH	Principal as decision-maker. Decisions are reactive to state, district, and federal mandates.	A shared-decision making structure is put into place and discussions begin on how to achieve a school vision. Most decisions are focused on solving problems and are reactive.	Leadership team is committed to continuous improvement. Leadership seeks inclusion of all school sectors and supports study teams by making time provisions for their work.	Leadership team represents a true shared decision-making structure. Study teams are reconstructed for the implementation of a comprehensive continuous improvement plan.	A strong continuous improvement structure is set into place that allows for input from all sectors of the school, district, and community, ensuring strong communication, flexibility, and refinement of approach and beliefs. The school vision is student focused, based on data and appropriate for school/community values, and meeting student needs.
IMPLEMENTATION	Principal makes all decisions, with little or no input from teachers, the community, or students. Leadership inspects for mistakes.	School values and beliefs are identified; the purpose of school is defined; a school mission and student learning standards are developed with representative input. A structure for studying approaches to achieving student learning standards is established.	Leadership team is active on study teams and integrates recommendations from the teams' research and analyses to form a comprehensive plan for continuous improvement within the context of the school mission. Everyone is kept informed.	Decisions about budget and implementation of the vision are made within teams, by the principal, by the leadership team, and by the full staff as appropriate. All decisions are communicated to the leadership team and to the full staff.	The vision is implemented and articulated across all grade levels and into feeder schools. Quality standards are reinforced throughout the school. All members of the school community understand and apply the quality standards. Leadership team has systematic interactions and involvement with district administrators, teachers, parents, community, and students about the school's direction.
OUTCOME	Decisions lack focus and consistency. There is little staff buy-in. Students and parents do not feel they are being heard. Decision-making process is clear and known.	The mission provides a focus for all school improvement and guides the action to the vision. The school community is committed to continuous improvement. Quality leadership techniques are used sporadically.	Leaders are seen as committed to planning and quality improvement. Critical areas for improvement are identified. Faculty feel included in shared decision making.	There is evidence that the leadership team listens to all levels of the organization. Implementation of the continuous improvement plan is linked to student learning standards and the guiding principles of the school. Teachers are empowered.	Site-based management and shared-decision making truly exists. Teachers understand and display an intimate knowledge of how the school operates. Teachers support and communicate with each other in the imple-mentation of quality strategies. Teachers implement the vision in their classrooms and can determine how their new approach meets student needs and leads to the attainment of student learning standards.

Education for the Future Initiative, Chico CA (1994). Rev. 3/99

Table A6
Partnership Development

	ONE	TWO	THREE	FOUR	FIVE
APPROACH	There is no system for input from parents, business, or community. Status quo is desired for managing the school.	Partnerships are sought, but mostly for money and things.	School has knowledge of why partnerships are important and seeks to include businesses and parents in a strategic fashion related to student learning standards for increased student achievement.	School seeks effective win-win business and community partnerships and parent involvement to implement the vision. Desired outcomes are clearly identified. A solid plan for partnership development exists.	Community, parent, and business partnerships become integrated across all student groupings. The benefits of outside involvement are known by all. Parent and business involvement in student learning is refined. Student learning regularly takes place beyond the school walls.
IMPLEMENTATION	Barriers are erected to close out involvement of outsiders. Outsiders are managed for least impact on status quo.	A team is assigned to get partners and to receive input from parents, the community, and business in the school.	Involvement of business, community, and parents begins to take place in some classrooms and after school hours related to the vision. Partners begin to realize how they can support each other in achieving school goals. School staff understand what partners need out of the partnership.	There is a systematic utilization of parents, community, and businesses schoolwide. Areas in which the active use of these partnerships benefits student learning are clear.	Partnership development is articulated across all student groupings. Parents, community, business, and educators work together in an innovative fashion to increase student learning and to prepare students for the 21st Century. Partnerships are evaluated for continuous improvement.
OUTCOME	There is little or no involvement of parents, business, or community at large. School is a closed, isolated system.	Much effort is given to establishing partnerships. Some spotty trends emerge, such as receiving donated equipment.	Some substantial gains are achieved in implementing partnerships. Some student achievement increases can be attributed to this involvement.	Gains in student satisfaction with learning and school are clearly related to partnerships. All partners benefit.	Previously non-achieving students enjoy learning, with excellent achievement. Community, business, and home become common places for student learning, while school becomes a place where parents come for further education. Partnerships enhance what the school does for students.

Education for the Future Initiative, Chico CA (1994). Rev. 3/99

Table A7
Continuous Improvement and Evaluation

	ONE	TWO	THREE	FOUR	FIVE
APPROACH	Neither goals nor strategies exist for the evaluation and continuous improvement of the school organization or for elements of the school organization.	The approach to continuous improvement and evaluation is problem solving. If there are no problems, or if solutions can be made quickly, there is no need for improvement or analyses. Changes in parts of the system are not coordinated with all other parts.	Some elements of the school organization are evaluated for effectiveness. Some elements are improved on the basis of the evaluation findings.	All elements of the school's operations are evaluated for improvement and to ensure congruence of the elements with respect to the continuum of learning students experience.	All aspects of the school organization are rigorously evaluated and improved on a continuous basis. Students, and the maintenance of a comprehensive learning continuum for students, become the focus of all aspects of the school improvement process.
IMPLEMENTATION	With no overall plan for evaluation and continuous improvement, strategies are changed by individual teachers and administrators only when something sparks the need to improve. Reactive decisions and activities are a daily mode of operation.	Isolated changes are made in some areas of the school organization in response to problem incidents. Changes are not preceded by comprehensive analyses, such as an understanding of the root causes of problems. The effectiveness of the elements of the school organization, or changes made to the elements, is not known.	Elements of the school organization are improved on the basis of comprehensive analyses of root causes of problems, client perceptions, and operational effectiveness of processes.	Continuous improvement analyses of student achievement and instructional strategies are rigorously reinforced within each classroom and across learning levels to develop a comprehensive learning continuum for students and to prevent student failure.	Comprehensive continuous improvement becomes the way of doing business at the school. Teachers continuously improve the appropriateness and effectiveness of instructional strategies based on student feedback and performance. All aspects of the school organization are improved to support teachers' efforts.
OUTCOME	Individuals struggle with system failure. Finger pointing and blaming others for failure occurs. The effectiveness of strategies is not known. Mistakes are repeated.	Problems are solved only temporarily and few positive changes result. Additionally, unintended and undesirable consequences often appear in other parts of the system. Many aspects of the school are incongruent, keeping the school from reaching its vision.	Evidence of effective improvement strategies is observable. Positive changes are made and maintained due to comprehensive analyses and evaluation.	Teachers become astute at assessing and in predicting the impact of their instructional strategies on individual student achievement. Sustainable improvements in student achievement are evident at all grade levels, due to continuous improvement.	The school becomes a congruent and effective learning organization. Only instruction and assessment strategies that produce quality student achievement are used. A true continuum of learning results for all students.

Education for the Future Initiative, Chico CA (1994). Rev. 3/99

Appendix B
Mechanics of Putting Together a School Portfolio

Mechanics of Putting a School Portfolio Together

Headers and Footers

Headers and footers not only give the portfolio a professional look, they also make it clear to the reader which pages are the narrative, and which are other evidence you have added. If you have a logo, you can import it into the header so that it will print on every page. Otherwise, a simple header with the school name can be easily created in most word processing programs. Color in the heading is very attractive and easy to achieve if you have a color printer.

The following example, uses shading over white letters:

River Road Elementary School

An interesting font with a line under the school name is another alternative:

River Road Elementary   *School Portfolio*

Fonts, Justification, and Margins

We recommend a font that has serifs, such as Palatino. Serifs are the little curls at the end of letters or the feet on letters. Use a common font so that the person who updates the portfolio next year doesn't have to hunt for the font you used. We also recommend justifying the type on both the left and right, so that it looks like the print in a book. Wide margins are not only visually pleasing but also make it easy to distinguish the narrative pages, and make it easy for others to write their input on the draft version. Whatever you choose, use it consistently throughout the narrative pages.

Inserting Photos

Using a digital camera makes it easy to import pictures right into the word-processed document. If you use traditional film, you have the choice of scanning and importing images, or simply pasting the photo right into a space in the text. While many word-processing programs are now like desktop publishing programs in that they allow for flow-around text, we often use photos that are 4 by 6 inches set horizontally in 6 inch-wide text.

Page Numbering

Number the narrative pages (the pages written specifically for the portfolio) within each section or chapter of the portfolio. Use the section name or number with the page number to indicate where the page belongs. For example, the third page in Information and Analysis would have that section name at the bottom, followed by Page 3. Numbering within each section allows for changes to the section without reprinting the entire portfolio.

Adding Evidence

In addition to the narrative pages, there are a variety of artifacts that you will want to include. These are discussed at the end of each section. These can either not be numbered at all, or can be numbered with the preceding page and a letter (e.g., 5-A) Some schools use a different color paper to photocopy evidence.

Tabs

In addition to the seven main sections of the portfolio, many schools create subsections. For example, behind Information and Analysis you might have sub-sections entitled demographics, questionnaires, and student achievement data. You might also have subsections within these, depending on what data you have collected. You can make the subsection distinct from the main sections by using upper case vs. lower case letters, or by using tabs that look different.

Protecting the Portfolio

School portfolios seem to be used most often during the times when staff or community members have food in their hands! We recommend laminating or using plastic page protectors on all pages to keep them clean.

Notes

Notes

Notes

Notes

Notes

Notes

Notes

References and Resources

References and Resources

Mapping the Route to Education Excellence

The references used in this book, along with other resources that will assist busy school administrators and teachers in continuously improving, appear below.

Barker, J. (1993). *Discovering the future: The business of paradigms*. New York, NY: HarperBusiness.

Bean, W. (1993). *Strategic planning that makes things happen: Getting from where you are to where you want to be*. Amherst, MA: HRD Press, Inc.

Bernhardt, V.L. (1998). *Data Analysis for Comprehensive Schoolwide Improvement*. Larchmont, NY: Eye on Education, Inc.

Bernhardt, V.L. (1999, June). *Databases Can Help Teachers with Standards Implementation*. Invited Monograph No. 5. California Association for Supervision and Curriculum Development (CASCD).

Bernhardt, V.L. (1999). *Designing and Using Databases for School Improvement*. Larchmont, NY: Eye on Education, Inc.

Bernhardt, V.L. (1998, March). *Multiple Measures*. Invited Monograph No. 4. California Association for Supervision and Curriculum Development (CASCD).

Bernhardt, V.L. (1998). *The School Portfolio: A Comprehensive Framework for School Improvement*. Second Edition. Larchmont, NY: Eye on Education, Inc.

Collins, C. C. & Porras, J. I. (1991). Organizational Vision and Visionary Organizations. *California Management Review Reprint Series*. Fall. pp. 30-51.

Covey, S. R. (1991). *Principle-centered leadership*. New York, NY: Fireside.

Covey, S. R. (1989). *The 7 habits of highly effective people: Powerful lessons in personal change*. New York, NY: Fireside.

Covey, S. R., Merrill, A. R. & Merrill, R. R. (1994). *First things first: To live, to love, to learn, to leave a legacy.* New York, NY: Simon & Schuster.

Deal, T. & Peterson, K. (1994). *The leadership paradox: Balancing logic and artistry in school.* San Francisco, CA: Jossey-Bass Inc.

Deming, W. E. (1993). *The new economics for industry, government, education.* Cambridge, MA: Massachusetts Institute of Technology Center for Advanced Engineering Study.

Deming, W. E. (1982). *Out of the crisis.* Cambridge, MA: Massachusetts Institute of Technology Center for Advanced Engineering Study.

Drucker, P. (1993). *Innovation and entrepreneurship: Practice and principles.* New York, NY: HarperBusiness.

Fullan, M. (1993). *Changing Forces: Probing the depths of educational reform.* Bristol, PA: Falmer.

Glasser, W. (1992). *The quality school: managing students without coercion.* New York, NY: HarperCollins Publishers.

Glasser, W. (1993). *The quality school teacher: A companion volume to the quality school.* New York, NY: HarperCollins Publishers.

Glickman, C. D. (1993). *Renewing America's schools: A guide for school-based action.* San Francisco, CA: Jossey-Bass Publishers.

Hamilton-Merritt, J. (1993). *Tragic Mountains: The Hmong, the Americans, and the secret wars for Laos, 1942-1992.* Indiana University Press.

Joyce, B. (Ed.). (1990). *Changing school culture through staff development.* Alexandria VA: Association for Supervision and Curriculum Development.

Joyce, B., Wolf, J., & Calhoun, E. (1993). *The self-renewing school.* Alexandria VA: Association for Supervision and Curriculum Development.

Kovalik, S. with Olsen, K. D. (1992). *Integrated thematic instruction: the model.* Village of Oak Creek, AZ: Susan Kovalik & Associates.

Lezotte, L. (1997). *Learning for all.* Okemos, MI: Effective Schools Products, Ltd.

Lindsay, J. (1999) *The Hmong People in the U.S.* http://www.athenet.net/~jlindsay/Hmong_tragedy.html.

Lynch, R. & Werner, T. (1992). Continuous improvement: Teams & tools. Atlanta, GA: QualTeam, Inc.

National LEADership Network Study Group on Restructuring Schools, U.S. Department of Education. (1991). *Developing leaders for restructuring schools: New habits of mind and heart.* Washington, D.C.: United States Department of Education.

National LEADership Network Study Group on Restructuring Schools, U.S. Department of Education. (1993). *Toward quality in education: The leader's odyssey.* Washington, D.C.: United States Department of Education.

Peters, T. (1987). *Thriving on chaos: A handbook for a management revolution.* New York, NY: HarperPerrenial.

Senge, P., Kleiner, A., Roberts, C., Ross, R., Roth, G., Smith, B. (1999). *The dance of change: The challenges of sustaining momentum in learning organizations.* New York, NY: Doubleday Currency.

Senge, P. (1990). *The fifth discipline: The art & practice of the learning organization.* New York, NY: Doubleday Currency.

Townsend, P. L. with Gebhardt, J. E. (1990). *Commit to quality.* New York, NY: John Wiley & Sons, Inc.

Von Blanckensee, L. (1999). *Technology tools for young learners.* Larchmont, NY: Eye on Education, Inc.

WWW Hmong Webpage. (1999). http://www.hmongnet.org/

Index

Index